MORE Than 2 PATHS

Biblical Secrets to Living Your Most Fulfilling LGBTQIA Life

MORE Than 2 PATHS

Biblical Secrets to Living Your
Most Fulfilling LGBTQIA Life
or
Beyond Either/Or Thinking to Fulfilling
Same-Sex Connections That Last

Karl W. Beckstrand, M.A.

Cover portrait by Mathew C. Judd.
Interior print design and layout by Sydnee Hyer

The author wishes to extend special thanks to Chris, A.J, Adrianne, Anna, Brian, Michele, Robert, Scott, Susan, and Heather.

Published by Paths Press (an imprint of Premio Publishing), Midvale, UT, USA. Order direct, or via any major distributor
PremioBooks.com

Library of Congress Catalog Number: 2022937790

ISBN: 978-1951599157

For Anthony, Caton, Cesar, Chance, Chris, David,
Eduardo, George, Jose, Kim, Leo, Mark
Michael, Patrick, Rick, Saeed, Shane,
Shawn, Steve, Stephen, and Zach

Table of Contents

Jump in Here!

CLOSE BEYOND IMAGINATION

OUR GREATEST JOYS COME VIA RELATIONSHIPS. For decades, I dreamed of deep, lasting human connection, only to experience repeated disappointment. Somewhere in my twenties, I concluded that I'd have to wait for heaven to enjoy that kind of bonding with others. But God is more generous than we often give Him credit for; today, I feel my relationships are more profound, stable, and rewarding than I had dreamed possible, and perhaps more than most people do. Turns out, I only had to let go of the poor ways of relating and leave behind the unhelpful ideas that I'd clung to. I'd like to share with you how you might have this contentment as well.

More than a third of Americans say they are chronically lonely.[1] Achieving lasting, happy relationships is a challenge for just about anyone; for LGBTQIA people, it can seem impossible.

People often see only binary options, including in relationships; gay culture has *generally* viewed (nonfamilial) same-sex relationships as being either superficial or sexual. Simplistic views reduce our available options and minimize our chances for deep connection

Yet, there are infinite ways to be human, to relate as humans, let alone as LGBTQIA individuals. There may be better ways to love and be loved, regardless of orientation, than the standard ways the world often signals.[2] I'm convinced that God made *all* men—heterosexual *and* gay—with the capacity to love each other intensely and lastingly. I believe women enjoy this same blessing. Activities segregated by sex in history were not always driven by mores; men often prefer the company of men, and women often prefer to associate with other women.

I'm not typically someone who publishes intimate details of my life, but I feel that what I've learned is too important not to share. Most of my words are directed to people with same-sex attraction—this term is used here, instead of "gay," to include people, like me, who are also attracted to the opposite sex (*bisexual* or *bi*). My experience is individual and comes from a male perspective, and some of what I say may not apply to all same-sex–attracted people. While I address families and friends of LGBTQIA people in the epilogue, I hope anyone—especially spouses of LGBTQIA people—will gain perspective from this entire book.

Is someone you love struggling with their faith over LGBTQIA questions or conflicts? Are you? This book offers perspective and insights that can bolster confidence in God's tender provision for every soul. God loves every individual.

There is divine purpose for our differences. As we begin to see as God sees, we gain appreciation for ourselves and others—perhaps especially because of our differences.[3]

I've found that people can easily read their own story as they peruse mine. If what you read here seems very much like your story, consider that, besides learning from the experiences we share, you can absorb insight from what is unique about my story.

If you're usually a fast reader or you like to leapfrog through chapters, I'd invite you to slow your usual pace for this book. Sitting a while with concepts can prevent misunderstanding, and sometimes the mind needs time to mull over new perspectives. It's okay if you don't agree with me, though I hope you'll keep these thoughts in mind for future insight. Keeping one's options open allows the greatest possibility for fulfilment.[4]

Is this a "change" book? Yes—but not in the way you might think. This book deals with changes that all people could benefit from (and the change isn't in sexual orientation). Rather than reduce opportunities for love, I wish to deepen and extend love's unique expressions to a variety of spheres.

Chapter notes reflect my particular faith tradition and might not represent yours. I hope you'll find them fascinating if not fortifying to your faith in God and your devotion to Him.[5]

The discussion of human interpersonal relationships, including sexuality, is constantly expanding and shifting. Terminology changes. In the space of my own life, I've seen many terms emerge and fall out of fashion. There are terms that I still use out of habit or because they're comfortable for me. To provide clarity as I tell my story, I've provided definitions here of terms I use frequently. The appendixes offer more information.

DEFINITIONS

- For the purposes of this book, *having sex* and *being sexual* refer broadly to ways of interacting with people that typically lead to sexual climax.
- *Sex* (biological) and *gender* (societal/cultural) are technically not synonyms, but I use them interchangeably in this book (except when *sex* refers to coitus or sexual stimulation) because that's generally how they're used by laypeople.
- The *Q* in LGBTQIA can stand for "queer" (which is sometimes used broadly here, like gay, to refer to any LGBTQIA person), but it can also stand for "questioning" (see Appendix B).
- *I* in LGBTQIA stands for "intersex" (previously known as *hermaphrodite*).
- *A* at the end of LGBTQIA represents "asexual." Asexuals use *ace* for short.

One important aspect of learning to think about things in new ways is learning how to talk about ideas differently. Learning and using new terminology, or repurposing old terms, might feel awkward or even uncomfortable at first. But using respectful and appropriate terminology is one way of showing love and respect for all and for the differences in our journeys. I'm still learning this, but more precise use of language helps us break out of confining, binary ways of thinking that prevent us from finding the love and happiness we are meant to enjoy. [5]

> *"The goal is not to change who you are*
> *but to become more of who you are at your best."* [6]
>
> —Sally Hogshead

NOTES

1. Richard Weissbourd et al., "Loneliness in America: How the Pandemic Has Deepened an Epidemic of Loneliness and What We Can Do about It," Making Caring Common Project, Harvard Graduate School of Education, last modified February 2021, https://mcc.gse.harvard.edu/reports/loneliness-in-america. Prior to COVID-19, a Cigna survey said 3 of 5 people are lonely. Elena Renken, "Most Americans Are Lonely, And Our Workplace Culture May Not Be Helping," National Public Radio, January 23, 2020, https://www.npr.org/sections/health-shots/2020/01/23/798676465/most-americans-are-lonely-and-our-workplace-culture-may-not-be-helping. See also "Why Men Are Lonelier in America Than Elsewhere," *The Economist*, January 1, 2022, https://www.economist.com/united-states/2022/01/01/why-men-are-lonelier-in-america-than-elsewhere; "Donate: Help the Foundation for Male Studies Meet Its Objective," Foundation for Male Studies, https://www.malestudies.org/donate.

2. Most of us delicately try to hold both truth and love (I doubt any of us do it perfectly)—one virtue without the other can be a vice. I did write a book, the subtitle of which is *Communication Guaranteed Not to Offend.* This is not that book—and *that* book was a gag, since such communication seems to elude us mortals.
3. Isa. 55:8; 1 Sam. 16:7.
4. Some people tell me they have explored the kind of connectedness I discuss in this book without seeing a payoff. When I probe, they acknowledge that they tried to combine two inadequate ways of relating (or never truly let go of old ways of relating). To truly experience profound and resilient connection, some things are best let go or avoided.
5. See https://PremioBooks.com/joy for expanded notes and active links (see QR code at the end of the book). All biblical references are to the King James Version. I include references to books of The Church of Jesus Christ of Latter-day Saints. Sections and verses of the Doctrine and Covenants are shown in the format "D&C 19:23," while abbreviations in the Book of Mormon and the Pearl of Great Price are as follows:

1 Nephi	1 Ne.
2 Nephi	2 Ne.
Jacob	Jac.
Jarom	Jar.
Mosiah	Mos.
Helaman	Hel.
Moroni	Moro.
Abraham	Abr.

Fiona and Terryl Givens in their book, *All Things New: Rethinking Sin, Salvation, and Everything In Between* (Meridian: Faith Matters Publishing, 2020), offer new ideas on traditional terminology. The chapter titles alone give a wealth of new perspectives on old language:

- Salvation: From Rescue to Realization
- Heaven: From "Where" to "with Whom"
- Fall: From Corruption to Ascension
- Obedience: From Subject to Heir
- Sin: From Guilt to Woundedness
- Justice: From Punishment to Restoration
- Forgiveness: From Transactional Love to Absolute Love
- Atonement: From Penal-Substitution to Radical Healing
- Worthiness: From Merit to Miracle
- Church: From Reservoir of the Righteous to Collaborators with Christ.

See also "Big Question #6: What about Our LGBT Brothers and Sisters?" Faith Matters, n.d., https://faithmatters.org/big-question-6-what-about-our-lgbt-brothers-and-sisters/; Garrett R. Maxwell, "The Good God Hermeneutic: A Reconsideration of Religious Vocabulary," *Interpreter: A Journal of Latter-day Saint Faith and Scholarship* 47 (2021): 151–58, https://archive.bookofmormoncentral.org/content/good-god-hermeneutic-reconsideration-religious-vocabulary.

6. Sally Hogshead, Quotss.com, SoftCopy IT Services Pvt. Ltd., accessed August 17, 2022, http://www.quotss.com/quote/The-goal-is-not-to-change-who-you-are-but-to-become-more-of-who-you-are-at.

7. As not everyone is comfortable with the world knowing their personal situation or status, I have changed nearly all friends' names in this book, and I sometimes use the vague reference "personal social media post" (with the "names" and permission of the authors) where applicable.

CHAPTER 1

Out of Bounds

Why would you stay in an organization that doesn't want you? You're a repressed sheep—blindly following what a flawed preacher tells you to do. You should quit your church and live the way you want to live.

PEOPLE SAY THINGS LIKE THIS WHEN they learn I'm an active member of The Church of Jesus Christ of Latter-day Saints—and that I, a man, am attracted to both men and women.[1] I tend to smile and laugh it off, but few wounds go deeper than being misunderstood.

When people make these statements to me, they make assumptions about me and my relationship with my faith. What many people don't know is that my history *doesn't* reflect a habit of obedience to faith leaders, personal excitement for gay sex, or feeling rejected by my church because of my sexual orientation. Clearly, attraction to one's own sex doesn't mean the same path for everyone!

I have always wanted my own family and came close to marrying multiple times. In 2008, I ended an engagement to a woman with whom I wasn't compatible (she knew I was bisexual, but we had significant differences in other areas). At that time, my health was such that I told God I no longer had the energy to search for a wife (but if He wanted to drop the ideal woman in my lap, that would be fine).

It had been many years since I'd been sexual with a man, but because I had been sexually compulsive—out of control—for much of my early life, fear of falling back into that chaotic, destructive path caused me to become a recluse (not a great decision, but it was all I could think of at the time). It's tragic when two-option choices are all one can imagine!

I still had the friends I'd grown up with, but most were married and busy with growing families. Soon, a rift in my own family left me even more isolated.

While I know that sex can be fulfilling and lovely in ideal circumstances, I sensed that sex wasn't what I lacked. Based on my experiences, I felt sure that sex (in my case) would take me farther away from what I needed, but I had no idea how to find true connection.

This book is not about addiction—though sex addiction has given me key insights on broader topics. My experience informs me; you and your experience may not harmonize with mine, but I believe that the principles I've learned can be applied to a variety of experiences and circumstances to help people find fulfillment in all their same-sex relationships.

Today, I am no longer disconnected, but I'm not compulsive in my behavior, either. I love who I am—feelings and all! I don't experience shame regarding my attractions, I have incredibly deep long-term relationships, and I have peace with God about my worth in His sight.[2] But there is a lot more detail on how I came to appreciate and be blessed by *all* of my feelings.

POINTS TO PONDER

- Is Sexual Orientation a Choice? Sexual *orientation* is not a defect, it's not a sin, it's not contagious, it's not a mortal choice, and it's not an act of rebellion. People choose their actions, but feelings are not in our hands quite the same way. We can exert influence over feelings, but often, we simply feel what we feel. Note that sexual orientation is a set of feelings and impulses, while sex is a set of actions. We can learn to manage our feelings, but we do not choose the feelings themselves. Consider this: Why would anyone *choose* to be mostly attracted to a group where most of its members (men, in my case) would *not* reciprocate and might even react negatively to such attraction?
- Our greatest joys come via relationships, yet long-term relationship bliss is elusive, regardless of sexual orientation. I believe God's help is needed in *every* relationship.

- There is divine purpose for our differences. What might those purposes be? What about differences in our sexualities?
- Few choices are binary, and either/or options are often artificial when it comes to human relationships. There are infinite ways to be human, let alone LGBTQIA. There may be better ways to love and be loved (regardless of orientation) than the standard ways the world signals. In what ways can thinking beyond the binary open us to other blessings?

NOTES

1. The following is written by Blake Fisher, inclusion advisor at Brigham Young University:

   I'm curious if celibate, Buddhist monks [ever hear] the following:

   - It's so sad that your [tradition] "forces" you to give up sex and "makes" you live this way.
   - A loving God would never ask you to sacrifice anything that feels good or could make you happy.
   - Your life is going to be so sad and meaningless without a romantic, sexual relationship.
   - I can't believe your church tells you what to eat, what to wear, and how to live . . . so controlling.
   - Do you wonder if you're living this way because of fear . . . fear of rejection, of your own desires, of hell, the unknown?
   - I once knew someone who was a celibate monk, they were so much happier after they left, you should leave too.

- Don't worry, your church is eventually going to change (catch up with the times) . . . and then you'll be happy.
- Even if you've found peace and joy on your journey, it's probably best that you keep it to yourself so others don't feel pressured to live the same way. (Personal social media post, 2022)

2. John 3:17; Mark 12:30.

CHAPTER 2
Either/Or?

The first great commandment . . . to the human family: to love God . . . without . . . compromise . . . with all our heart, might, mind, and strength. . . . But the first great truth in the universe is that God loves us exactly that way—wholeheartedly, without reservation or compromise, with all of His heart, might, mind, and strength. And when those majestic forces from His heart and ours meet without restraint, there is a veritable explosion of spiritual, moral power. Then, as Teilhard de Chardin wrote, "for [the] second time in the history of the world, man will have discovered fire." [1]

—*Jeffrey R. Holland*

SO, YOU'RE GAY OR BISEXUAL OR otherwise queer. What does that look like for you? What does it mean? Perhaps you assumed or were told by a leader that to be a good Christian, you must avoid contact with those of your sex. If you've (rightly) concluded that you can't do that—that you somehow need those of your sex—will you leave your church? I have ample evidence that you, as a child of God, *do* need those of your sex and that you are *needed* among the believers (especially those of your own sex).[2]

Why talk about this? Author Meghan Decker says people can feel isolated by differences—hopeless. Some can't heal or even receive love, much less give love, until they feel that their core self is known and accepted. I have experienced this. Many people are still trying to figure out who they really are at their core. Until this happens, a counterproductive "us versus them" worldview can be difficult to shake. Whether you only need to "come out of the closet" to be honest with yourself or with others, know that coming out removes barriers, but it doesn't create wholeness on its own; there are wondrous options beyond this!

You are not in a separate class based on your feelings or your behavior—neither are you inferior to heterosexual people. They experience frustration, heartbreak, and pain as well; not everything always goes their way.[3] Decker explains that while isolation, shame, and hopelessness aren't inherent in being LGBTQIA, these feelings are often attached to these orientations:

> Why do I need to come out when I don't plan to leave the Church or my marriage—when I'm not changing anything? Because being honest and open does change everything. It relieves me of the shame that has shadowed my life for decades. This is especially important for members of the Church who may have internalized judgment, rejection, and shame. The incongruence between how we are seen and the inner reality of our lives is excruciating.

> We might feel we are deceiving those around us, both family and friends. We are afraid of the rejection we *might* feel if others saw us as we really are. Our perception of ourselves becomes dark and distorted. . . .
>
> After I came out publicly to my friends and family, I felt as though I could breathe deeply for the first time in my adult life. I didn't realize how tightly I held myself, and fear of discovery limited every relationship. I was friendly but fearful, caring yet careful. My family and friends have so much more of me now because I'm not hiding.[4]

SATAN'S FIRST COMMANDMENT: "HIDE!"[5]

The insights I'll be sharing with you have been hard-won through my experiences; through struggles with my beliefs, sexuality, addiction, and relationships; and, ultimately, through peace and fulfillment via deep connections and the grace of Jesus Christ. For background, I'll share with you some things about where I'm coming from.

My earthly paths opened up in San Jose, California. I love that one-time agricultural area that morphed into Silicon Valley before my eyes.

I was raised by a liberal mom (born a member of The Church of Jesus Christ [Latter-day Saint] but not active until converted as a teen) and a conservative, fourth-generation LDS dad. I won't detail the mutual rejection between my father and me; some people explain away homosexuality as being the result of a poor relationship with a same-sex parent, but I believe the explanations for same-sex attraction are multiple and complex, and I don't pretend to have a grasp on them. A lot of people attracted to their own sex had close, affectionate relationships with their same-sex parent. I did not.[6]

My mother had severe health challenges. My father resented having had a family, as his first love (he'd probably concede) was his motorcycle and the open road. His time and resources went to that love. My older siblings remember parents who loved each other. I remember warfare.

As the youngest of four kids, I was loved but neglected. My mom's health prevented her from seeing that we left the house "kempt." My dad's spending meant we occasionally went without food, clothing, or heat. The result was that I didn't always appear well cared for, and this invited rejection and abuse from peers (I was also not nimble or street smart).

When I was about 12 years old I poured my heart out to my dad in a letter, asking him to love me. He never acknowledged I'd even written him. Having said this, I cannot ignore the advantages I had growing up with a father present who usually provided for me and offered an example of work, sport, and creativity.

None of these things caught God by surprise; He knew all that I would feel and experience before I was even born![7]

My parents did succeed in giving me the most important advantage: a knowledge of Jesus Christ. I cannot overstate the value of what my mother taught me, often from her sickbed, about the gospel of peace. My father got me to church most Sundays.

While it was never an ideal existence, Hans Christian Andersen expressed well my life: "An invisible and fatherly heart has beat for me!"[8] As far back as I can remember, I have had a certainty of a Heavenly Father who loves me. There are gifts I do not possess, but one of my gifts is a sure knowledge of the reality of God and of His loving nature. For the most part, I didn't project my earthly father's flaws onto my Eternal Father.

From an early age, I noticed men with keen interest—though I didn't have sexual thoughts about them until sex was shown to me.

I was pulled into sexual activity by a male peer when I was eight years old.[9] I didn't want sexual interest in men, and I agonized about not being "normal." No one had instructed me on sex or on how to avoid premature sexual relating—certainly not with guys. Over the next decade, before my church mission, I was sexually active on and off. Looking back at my eight- to nineteen-year-old self, I admire my determination and (often futile) efforts to avoid sex, though it had been, I feel, thrust on me.

My parents separated when I was in the seventh grade. This was a great hardship, though my dad tried to bolster us while my mom was away. They got back together when I was in high school, but the battle raged on, and I was in no mood to be parented after having to fend for myself for most of my childhood.

While I have always been attracted to women, I didn't experience physical attraction for them until I was in my mid-to-late teens. People who have never experienced attraction to both sexes have a hard time believing that bisexuals/biromantics exist. We do! People who've never experienced *no* desire for sex have a hard time believing that asexual people exist, but they absolutely do.[10]

I am *not* asexual. As someone who is mostly attracted to my own sex, I lived much of my life believing I had two choices:

1. Engage in gay sex and perhaps settle down with a gay partner
2. Marry someone of the opposite sex and try to find happiness in "straight" life

Both of these options left me wanting for something that I intuited was important to my life and my happiness. Only later would I grasp that *most* choices involve far more than two options![11]

In this book, I won't comment on whether God made me bi in orientation or whether God makes people gay; I don't know. What I do know is that God has *never* been taken by surprise by anything we experience. It follows that His plan for me has always included a path to Him where I could truly benefit from *all* of my experiences—blissful and painful. It's what Heavenly Father does: He takes what our enemy hopes will hurt us, and then He turns it for our good. I hope you'll see many examples of this in my story and see similar patterns in your own life.[12]

While I had some nurturing men in my life, they were so rare they felt almost nonexistent. Based on how I was treated by peers, I didn't consider myself good-looking. Aside from sexual partners, I was mostly a loner as a child.

One thing I consistently desired but didn't get much of (other than from my mom) was physical touch and affection. Our culture already minimizes and even discourages touch, especially among males, but societal aversion to homosexuality and recent health scares have exacerbated people's fears; we generally don't share enough physical touch.

When I was growing up, men with the greatest same-sex emotional needs could typically only find connection with gay men, and in my experience, there was usually a price for affection. The expectation is generally if you want touch and connection, you must be willing for the encounter to become sexual. I recall being a young man about to get sexual with a man, but wishing only to be held. True, I *was* a youth bursting with hormones, but the pity was that I was unaware of men who might connect with me in non-sexual ways. Though I often wanted simple affection, I felt obligated to be sexual; it seemed the only path to connect with a man. Otherwise, my life seemed to consist mostly of rejection.

Ugh—I'm evil! I'm disgusting! Repent. To say that telling my bishop about my sexual deeds filled me with terror would be an understatement. What if my family and peers found out? That could escalate ill treatment in a big way.

I feared being cast out, shunned. I'd never heard of a minor being excommunicated, but (I speculated) that must have been because no kid had done the things that I had! So often, our fears are a baseless waste of energy. Eventually, my desire for a clean conscience won. It wasn't a one-and-done confession, but my bishops were kind, and terror instantly transformed to relief and peace.[13]

Finally, in high school, I found friends and skills that boosted my confidence. I wasn't a jock (I was always puny until a growth spurt my senior year, when I discovered volleyball), though I enjoyed art and had leading roles in school plays.

It's fortunate that there was no public internet when I was young, or I may have hooked up with a lot more men before my mission and perhaps would have been too enmeshed in sex to believe it possible to give up. I remember at age eighteen going to a room alone and declaring—not to God, but to the devil—that I would qualify to serve a mission for Jesus Christ no matter what! While my determination was admirable, God knew I could not do it—alone.

My church leaders were gentle and supportive of my goal to serve a mission. They assured me of my worth and expressed confidence in my abilities. I recognize that not everyone in my situation gets such love; my heart aches for any that don't.

After a period of abstinence, medical exams, and having my wisdom teeth out, I said goodbye to friends and family in California. In the Provo, Utah, Church of Jesus Christ Missionary Training Center, a professional counselor who knew of my past challenged me to not be sexual with self or others for the entire two years of my mission. I committed—and learned an eternal secret that would help me later (once I understood it). I successfully served among the wonderful people of Chile while keeping my personal covenant of no sexual behavior. The key, which I didn't know at the time, was that when we covenant with God, He can make us capable of things we could never do on our own.

In South America we missionaries saw thousands of people embrace Christ's message. I learned that God's love is tenacious. I witnessed miracles (especially when I, a non-native Spanish speaker, could first understand the rapid Chilean speech and vernacular!). I gained an appreciation for US freedoms while living under a dictatorship. I distributed food, helped build a house, and got in-person training from Apostles. I saw lives transformed and people literally lifted out of slums. I gained lifelong friendships with some of the most generous people on earth. More than anything, I had a profound and personal assurance that I was doing the most important work on the planet. The contentment that comes from missionary service is easy to understand but difficult to describe.[14]

What I didn't realize is that a double course of antibiotics when my wisdom teeth were pulled had left my body defenseless and exposed in a microbial environment that was brand new to me. I got sick almost monthly; my body couldn't stand against the "new" invaders. The consequences of this assault would impact future options and change my life forever.

POINTS TO PONDER

- This book may have a different conclusion than you anticipate. What expectations or biases are you bringing into your reading?
- Many kids who were molested by someone of the same sex never become gay, and many who weren't molested do. What other misconceptions about the "causes" of homosexuality have you encountered?
- Bisexuals really are attracted to both sexes; asexual people really don't want sex.
- God knew what we would experience before we were born. His plan has always been that we would benefit from it all. In what ways have you benefitted from experiences that weren't obviously positive?

NOTES

1. Jeffrey R. Holland, "The Greatest Possession," *Liahona*, November 2021, 9, https://www.churchofjesuschrist.org/study/general-conference/2021/10/12holland?lang=ase. Deut. 30:6; Luke 10:27; Mark 12:30; Matt. 22:37; D&C 4:2, 59:5; Alma 39:13.
2. Rom. 3:23; Eph. 4.
3. 1 Cor. 12:21.
4. Meghan Decker, *Tender Leaves of Hope: Finding Belonging as LGBTQ Latter-day Saint Women* (Springville, UT: Cedar Fort, 2022), introduction, https://meghandecker.com/blog.
5. Gen. 3:6–11; Moses 4:5–19.
6. I nearly drowned three times as a child. My father once tried

to teach me to swim without communicating that to me. As he took me into the deep end of a pool with no explanation, I panicked and fought wildly to get back into the shallow. Because of my previous experiences with water, I experienced real terror. My father experienced huge rejection: His own son didn't trust him with his safety. I imagine this cemented his defensive rejection of me that began with me pushing him away years earlier as a baby. All I anticipated from him was a volatile temperament (mostly just his raised voice). I eventually taught myself to swim when I was about ten.

7. Job 21:22; Deut. 32:8; Isa. 42:9, 46:9, 48:3; Jer. 1:5; Acts 2:23, 17:26; Rom. 8:29, 11:2; 1 Pet. 1:2; Abr. 2:8.
8. Fredrik Böök, *Hans Christian Andersen: A Biography* (Norman: University of Oklahoma, 1962).
9. Based on what he knew at such a young age, I later concluded that the boy who introduced me to sex had previously been molested. I make no declarations about a connection between molestation and sexual orientation here. Many kids who are molested by someone of their sex never become gay, and many who aren't molested do. (Parents: Six or seven years is not too early an age to begin to discuss sex and boundaries with your child, so long as you tailor the conversation to a child's understanding.) See Gregory M. Herek, "Facts about Homosexuality and Child Molestation," LGBPsychology.org, n.d., https://lgbpsychology.org/html/facts_molestation.html; "Recognizing the Gift of Being Same-Sex Attracted: An Interview with SSA Women," Leading Saints, February 22, 2020, https://leadingsaints.org/recognizing-the-gift-of-being-same-sex-attracted-an-interview-with-ssa-women/; Kurt Freund, Robin Watson, and Robert Dickey, "Does Sexual Abuse in Childhood

Cause Pedophilia: An Exploratory Study," *Archives of Sexual Behavior* 19 (1990): 557–68, https://pubmed.ncbi.nlm.nih.gov/2082860/; "Same-Sex Attraction is Real," My Chosen Road (blog), February 16, 2020, http://mychosenroad.com/ssa-is-real/.

10. See "Overview," The Asexual Visibility & Education Network, n.d., https://www.asexuality.org/?q=overview.html.
11. Most choices involve *multiple* options, though we sometimes need practice seeing them. See Chip Heath and Dan Heath, *Decisive: How to Make Better Choices in Life and Work* (New York: Crown Business, 2013).
12. Gen. 50:20.
13. Neither the scriptures nor The Church of Jesus Christ of Latter-day Saints condemn same-sex love (same-sex love is a gift), only sexual relationships between anyone not in wife-husband marriage. My church doesn't base its stance on homosexuality on Bible verses alone. See Amos 3:7 and https://www.churchofjesuschrist.org/topics/gay?lang=eng.
14. You may not serve a mission, but if you have the opportunity to travel—take it! It may be the best education a person can receive. I've been privileged to visit many places—and I value those experiences over all advanced degrees.

CHAPTER 3

The Beaten Path

When the subject of temptation is discussed, inevitably there's someone who asks, "Why don't people simply exert willpower?" Aside from the obvious fault-finding of the weak-willed person, the other part of the question is "If God can make us stronger, why can't we just ask for a stronger will and be done with it?" Consider this, then: How many aspects of living the gospel are that simple?

AFTER THE HIGHS AND SUCCESSES OF my mission, I experienced the return of old struggles. Once I was back in the USA, I experienced more gut discomfort, but I worked while I waited for acceptance to Brigham Young University. In Utah, I lived with my oldest brother and three or four other roommates. I was excited to be living college life, but I was white-knuckling my way through lust, naively relying on my own strength and willpower.

Willpower is deceptive; it gives the illusion that we are in control—until we realize it is insufficient. Willpower generally fails, perhaps not immediately, but always eventually; it can never be a person's ultimate strength.[1]

C. S. Lewis spoke of a kind of existence that I experienced while white-knuckling myself into the closet (thinking, erroneously, it was where God wanted me):

> If you want to make sure of keeping it intact, you must give your heart to no one. . . . Wrap it carefully round with hobbies . . . avoid all entanglements; lock it up safe in the casket or coffin of your selfishness. But in that casket—safe, dark, motionless, airless—it will change. It will not be broken; it will become unbreakable, impenetrable, irredeemable. The alternative to tragedy, or at least to the risk of tragedy, is damnation. The only place outside Heaven where you can be perfectly safe from all the dangers and perturbations of love is Hell.[2]

Staying in the closet may seem safe, but there is a trapdoor in every closet—because what we're trying to hide from is a *God-given* need. When I was in the closet, I was all alone. I needed love, as all do (and I still need love!), but I was so determined to stay completely away from men to distance myself from temptation that I wasn't getting or giving any love at all. Closets, like C. S. Lewis's box, are dark and isolating. If we don't *step* out of closet doors, that trapdoor activates, we "fall off the wagon," and our illusion of control is lost, at least to a degree. The soul stamps and stomps until its needs are acknowledged—one way or another.[3]

PARADE OF ONE

Returning to California for the summer, I quickly and unexpectedly got sexual with a man I had just met, and I entered a spiral I could not get out of. Again, this didn't surprise God, especially considering the legitimate needs I was bottling up. By now, you're aware that I'm *not* talking about sexual needs. I had sincere emotional needs that weren't being met by "normal" socializing, but they weren't being met by my sexual relating, either.

Looking back to that time, I believe we can, in some aspects of our lives, unintentionally surrender our free will to the devil. I've experienced enough to know that just as there is a benevolent Higher Power, there is also a real being that takes delight in human misery. The devil absolutely knew I was miserable! He watched me flounder and fail, and he knew the depth of my need for human connection. I was trying so hard to meet my emotional needs, and the adversary took advantage of that situation by presenting me with options that were appealing but ultimately empty. Yet, the allure was real, and so I returned again and again.[4]

I tried to stop acting sexually; I'd mentally declare that I would never return to a certain hookup place, then would find myself there that very day. It's important to note that while I was acting compulsively with men, I was dating women, attending church, reading scriptures, fasting, and begging God daily to help me stop seeing guys. This went on for some time. My personal religious habits on their own—my actions of "righteousness"—couldn't save me from myself.

Because I hadn't been living morally, I was unable to return to BYU. Instead, I stayed in California and took community college classes, where I found many more sexual trysts. This wasn't simply twenty-two-year-old hormones; I could *not* stop acting out with men. I was relying on my willpower, and it clearly wasn't enough.

This was a frustrating time for me. I had felt successful, happy, and close to God while I was a missionary, but only a short while later, I was floundering in my attempts to be chaste. For two full years, I had kept my promise to abstain from sexual activity, so why was it so difficult now? Why did I feel so different? I understand now that God knew how alone I felt and that these experiences were important for me to sort out why and, eventually, how to meet my needs in healthful ways.

To clarify, in discussing the social-sexual aspects of life, I'm covering three scenarios:

1. God-given need to connect *emotionally* with those of my sex (the average person has this to some degree).[5]
2. Physical attraction to those of my own sex (regardless of whether it's related to #1).
3. Sexual behavior that is compulsive and at a higher frequency (often with a greater number of partners) than that of the average person. This last situation may not apply to many people. I am *not* saying

same-sex attraction is an addiction, only that my own behaviors around sex were compulsive.

So, what did I do as I slowly sorted out what was wrong with my life? I kept going to church. I kept praying, fasting, and reading the scriptures. I knew God was a god of miracles—and I needed a miracle. But I *felt* no help with my compulsive behavior.

I knew that the euphoria of sex wasn't giving me what I needed. The ironic thing is that as good as every orgasm felt, sex with men never was the relationship-cementing or fulfilling thing I'd been led to believe—though I *was* trying to meet some real male need. Even while dating men I cared for, I found that sexual activities failed to connect us in a way that helped satisfy; rather, they left me feeling *less* connected to my partner and unfulfilled in general. Yet, I kept coming back for more, hoping baselessly (every time) for that weld.

Some might argue that the emptiness was because of my culture, but keep in mind, I didn't get church or home chastity lessons until years *after* becoming sexually active—and those lessons were *not* about avoiding sex with men specifically. I never anticipated feeling ripped open emotionally by something that felt good physically. No adult had warned the youngster Karl that these experiences would leave me feeling hollow and low, so it's hard to attribute these empty feelings to cultural conditioning.

Guys intent on being sexual aren't easily persuaded against it. Yet, I hope that, if you find you feel as I did after engaging in sexual relations with those of your sex, you'll remember my experiences—and especially remember what I'm going to say about meeting one's real same-sex needs.

After months of confessions, my patient bishop suggested that I do what I swore I would never do: share my deepest secrets with more people. No! I was terrified, but I went to a counselor and suggested to him that I had a split personality: I was the stereotypical goody "Peter Priesthood," yet I was also a gay sex addict. He said I was simply one person with competing desires—and that conflicting desires are a normal part of being a human. Think of the desire-based choices you make every day; common conflicts include wanting to enjoy dessert every night versus wanting to keep trim, wanting to work to support family versus wanting to spend time with family, or wanting to complete a project versus wanting to sleep/read/watch movies/play games.

You might believe that a chunk of your life can be reduced to a struggle between your willpower and intense desires (and sometimes, those desires are contrary to your other goals); I hope to demonstrate that not only is there grace, power beyond your own, over seemingly overwhelming impulses, but also that as we meet real needs healthfully, life can be rich, and overwhelming urges can become fleeting—though illuminating—notions.[6]

For me, counseling wasn't enough. I needed peers I could identify with, people who understood my situation. The obvious obstacle was that it felt like any person who truly understood my situation wanted sex from me, and

I wanted it from them—or I wanted *something* from them. How could I get support?

One counselor introduced me to another gay Christian man in San Francisco who was also trying to be chaste. This gay man knew one other man in the same situation, and the three of us started meeting weekly in the capital of the gay world.

At first, I felt strong sexual attraction toward these men; then, I realized that I wanted to connect with them, relate to them on an emotional level. I'd learn later about the difference between wanting sex and the important impulse toward connection.

Here, though, is where I again experienced Christ's grace as I had as a missionary and—for the first time—recognized it as a power outside of my own, the *only* power that ever accomplished what I could not, especially where I had previously forfeited my will to my adversary. As I met with these men who also sought better relating through grace, something transformational occurred.

Week after week, we three "Freemen" talked, hugged, and went our separate ways without being sexual. It was years before I achieved real chastity, but these friendships marked a monumental shift for me. We three *truly* bonded; we're still in touch thirty-two years later and feel a special kinship. This unity is the result of a shared emotional and spiritual relationship, and in my experience, it's not typically preserved among people of the same sex who are sexual with each other.

By sharing my thoughts, actions, and feelings with others, I was demonstrating a sincere desire to be chaste, despite obvious weakness, and Christ was breaking chains that I had never been able to break on my own.[7]

This is what God does: Through His grace, He continually frees us and restores the agency of all who come to Him and speak their difficult truths. His grace is available to all because He loves us all.[8]

POINTS TO PONDER

- Are competing desires healthy? Like our need for food, emotional and social needs are God-given; they must be met and not suppressed. But sometimes our desires seem to be in competition. What can contrasting impulses teach us about our values and priorities?
- As true needs are met, seemingly overwhelming urges can become rare—though illuminating—notions, indicators that there are profound and positive reasons at the root of the desire. To what benefit might someone be attracted to their own sex?
- Willpower is one way we demonstrate our determination, but it cannot be our ultimate source of strength. Consider that grace is more than God's love or mercy; it's His divine enabling/transformative power, which He extends to us through the atoning sacrifice of Jesus Christ (2 Cor. 12:9; Ether

12:27). How have you experienced the interplay of your willpower and God's grace?

- Hiding our differences and difficulties may seem an easy solution, but doing so can lead to destructive isolation. Sharing differences and struggles with others can promote growth and bring liberating grace. What obstacles or fears hold you back from sharing your authentic self?
- God loves LGBTQIA persons! We are all His children. I celebrate queerness, including same-sex attraction, as part of His omniscient plan. Today, I no longer feel pressure to conform to my American or church culture. I don't care what people expect or think of me; I do what I believe is best, seeking to conform to God's will. How can you celebrate your queerness, or that of a loved one, in spite of social or cultural barriers?

NOTES

1. See Colleen Harrison, *He Did Deliver Me from Bondage* (Hyrum, UT: Windhaven, 2006), https://colleencharrison.com/books/he-did-deliver-me-from-bondage/. Harrison's book about overcoming addiction is based on principles of Christian discipleship in the Book of Mormon. See also https://www.bookofmormoncentral.org/.
2. C. S. Lewis, *The Four Loves* (Boston, New York: Mariner Books, 2012), 121.
3. While a wholly inadequate bandage, addiction is a sign that a legitimate need is not being met. "Jesus saw sin as wrong

but also was able to see sin as springing from deep and unmet needs on the part of the sinner." Spencer W. Kimball, "Jesus: The Perfect Leader," *Ensign*, August 1979, https://www.churchofjesuschrist.org/study/ensign/1979/08/jesus-the-perfect-leader?lang=eng.

4. Matt. 15:22; Mark 7:26; 2 Ne. 2:14, 18, 27. Satan cannot force us to do evil (or anything else), but we can give away our agency by doing as he suggests.
5. "God, as it seems to me, bestows two other gifts; a supernatural Need-love of Himself and a supernatural Need-love of one another." Lewis, *The Four Loves*, 129. "Heterosexual men commonly prefer the company of other men, in preference to the women with whom they may be romantically involved. This phenomenon is readily visible in the work environment, and graphically illustrated in recreational pursuits like drinking, gambling, and especially sports. Men's preference for men is based on a combination of positive identifications with [males]. . . . An almost universal fear of confrontation with inherent bisexuality dictates indirect expression of male-to-male intimacy. This is frequently in the form of activities culturally associated with masculinity and that affirm an often fragile sense of heterosexuality." Irwin Hirsch, "On Men's Preference for Men," *Gender and Psychoanalysis* 2, no. 4 (1997): 469–486, https://pep-web.org/browse/document/gap.002.0469a. See also Elwood David Watson, "Men Need Other Men in Their Lives!" The Good Men Project, October 26, 2016, https://goodmenproject.com/featured-content/men-need-men-lives-wcz/; Sarah K. McKenzie et al., "Masculinity, Social Connectedness, and Mental Health: Men's Diverse Patterns of Practice," *American*

Journal of Men's Health 12, no. 5 (September 2018): 1247–61, https://doi.org/10.1177/1557988318772732.

6. Acts 15:11; Eph. 2:8; 2 Cor. 12:9; Moro. 10:32.
7. "[Christ] could feed 5,000 *and there were leftovers.* 'My grace is sufficient for all men' (Ether 12:27). The Savior's redeeming and healing power can cover any sin, wound, or trial—no matter how large or how difficult—and there are leftovers. His grace is sufficient." Brent H. Nielson, "Is There No Balm in Gilead?" *Liahona*, November 2021, 58.
8. God loves queer persons! John 3:17; 1 Cor. 15:22; Luke 4:18. "The truth shall make you free." John 8:32. I have *not* condemned queerness (I celebrate it); I don't believe gays are defective or that queerness is a compulsion or a choice.

CHAPTER 4

Is It All About Sex?

God-given needs, like our need for sleep, are needs that God can help us fill in healthful ways—but He won't remove them.

NO MAN IS AN ISLAND

EVENTUALLY, I QUALIFIED TO RETURN TO BYU, then landed internships with a Massachusetts publisher and later in the US House of Representatives in Washington, DC. This all felt miraculous, as I was an atrocious student prior to college (I believe the Holy Spirit can increase our mental capacity).

After getting my undergraduate degree in journalism, I was recruited home to San Jose to work for a technical recruiting firm; it didn't hurt that I had worked in HR for Intel and Marriott during my long summers at home. Though my family had mostly moved to Utah, I returned to the Bay Area, where I made more friends, dated many women, and sang in a rock band.

I *started* to grasp that same-sex emotional needs are God-given to all people; for some people, they are greater than for others. Most women seem to understand this, but many men ignore it.

Earlier, I'd felt that God wasn't helping me, but now I was beginning to comprehend what was really happening. God won't remove my need for people any more than He'd remove my need for oxygen. Human social needs must be met in healthful ways. I believe many people are detrimentally isolated because their need continues to exist whether they reach out unsuccessfully, unhealthfully, or not at all. God isn't going to make things better if we don't seek positive ways to nourish one another socially.[1]

Our US culture often raises men and women to believe that once married, women can have bosom girlfriends they share everything with, but men should be content to have their wife be their world and only occasionally go running, golfing, or fishing with a buddy. Close, emotionally intimate friendships among adult men are viewed as suspect.[2]

My experience tells me that *unmet* God-given emotional needs—which are legitimate between men too—can easily be warped into chains by our enemy. In desperation to connect with others, and often not knowing exactly what it is we lack, we look to alternatives to fill that void. Compulsive behavior can be the result.

It's not just compulsive or promiscuous sexual behavior that arises: addictions to work, video games, pornography, food, gambling, shopping—and even excessive religiosity—are manifestations of *real* unmet emotional or social needs. You might see yourself here, but don't beat yourself up; you've been trying to meet real needs. This book offers better ways to do that. Addiction isn't simply recreational drug use or gaming; it is the soul seeking what it lacks: relief, purpose, nourishment, and bonding with others (not necessarily via sex).[3]

The biggest way God-given same-sex needs are turned against us is in the lie that they are *sexual* needs. We are not binary automatons with only two choices; there are more ways to connect with those of one's own sex than as a potential sexual partner or as a superficial associate—coworker, classmate, parishioner, neighbor.[4] I believe both attraction and admiration play a role in *any* friendship or social connection, whether the initial draw is intellectual, emotional, physical, or in mutual interests. In my experience, the fleeting connection of sex between people of the same sex cannot hold a candle to lasting, nonsexual bonds that seem only to deepen over the years.

When we understand that the void underlying every addiction is an unmet emotional need, we're better prepared to confront our own and other's addictions and compulsions. Some well-meaning people try to counter a loved one's addiction via isolation or by withdrawing connection. Unless continued interaction with the addict is detrimental to you, can you see how this is the wrong approach? Ask instead, "What are healthful, emotionally and spiritually nourishing ways to fill this chasm of need?"[5]

We all need love, affection, and healthy social connections. But is sex a need? More on that to come, but keep that question in mind during this brief discussion of attraction, promiscuity, and expectations of fidelity.

Most of us are familiar with the Kinsey scale used to measure sexual orientation; it has its flaws, but it's useful for a basic discussion. The Kinsey scale ranges from zero to six (*x* if one has no sexual attraction), zero being those physically attracted exclusively to the opposite sex (one hundred percent heterosexual) and six being those who are physically attracted exclusively to their own sex (one hundred percent homosexual). Many people are unaware of asexual people, or those who are *x* on the scale. Asexual people can be affectionate or not, attracted to the same or opposite sex, or somewhere in between, but they don't desire sex.[6]

Many one hundred percent "heterosexuals" or one hundred percent "homosexuals" find it difficult to believe someone could be somewhere in the middle of the scale, but a lot of us are. My attractions lean toward men, but my attraction to women puts me at about four on the scale; I have been a 3 at times, and other times a 5.

Gays, lesbians, bisexuals, and others fall all along the spectrum. Take a simple poll of your gay friends: Ask, "How would you feel about engaging in sex with the 'opposite' sex?" I've received a variety of answers. Feelings range from revulsion to apathy to attraction. This illustrates that not everyone experiences same-sex attraction in the same way.

This is all very useful to talk about sexual attraction, but what of emotional needs? I've seen no scale to measure the need to connect emotionally with one's own sex, but I imagine that need varies widely too. Mine is very strong; that I'm not a six on Kinsey's scale is a major indicator that the emotional need is distinct from physical attraction.

Apart from sex, there's an important lesson here: Healthful same-sex emotional interaction can be very fulfilling, yet emotional needs can *manifest* as sexual desire (regardless of sexual orientation). Have you ever thought you were hungry when you were actually dehydrated? If your need is water, eating more is never going to satisfy your thirst. Similarly, if we have long suppressed our need for emotional connection with those our own sex, it is possible to go overboard in pursuit of affection and get involved sexually. Just as food can't satisfy thirst, sex will never satisfy emotional deficits.

Unfortunately, a lot of people are unaware of the distinction between legitimate emotional need and the sex drive.[7] To exacerbate the situation, many of us have had unfortunate experiences that caused us to confuse sexual and emotional involvement. Others have been pursued romantically in extreme ways (or, at least, against their wills or protestations), so, sadly, a lot of people have learned to be emotionally *un*available.

Now that I am aware of a real need to connect *emotionally* with those of my sex and I've been relating with men in warm, healthful ways, my emotional needs are being satisfied, so sex with men is no longer the enticement for me that it used to be. It's been helpful to realize that "healthful ways" doesn't necessarily mean at arms' length. Just as our attractions to others differs, so too do the healthful solutions to meeting our emotional needs differ. Your own emotional needs and how to meet them may be different than mine.

For married people, it's important to remember that couples may be best served by encouraging their spouses (straight, gay, bi, or other) to meet legitimate same-sex *emotional* needs in healthful ways. Invite your spouse to have healthy friendships. Some guys are content to play ball together; some of us talk, share feelings, and hug. For those of us with strong same-sex emotional needs, these activities are vital.[8]

Meeting connection needs healthfully and regularly, with no sexual agenda, can illuminate our true needs to us, open previously unimagined relational possibilities, and greatly diminish selfish or unhealthful impulses toward others. It might also help with addictive behavior, reducing the draw of gaming, spending, pornography, masturbation, or overeating, because the emptiness that was there is now filled with satisfying human connection.

There's an elephant in the room: Sex feels very good. Sexual connection is satisfying while it lasts. What if you don't want sexual urges toward those of your sex to diminish? My sense is that people, generally, do want *something* better than a self-focused yearning: deep, lasting connection (the process toward which I cover in coming chapters). I suspect our culture is, generally, overfocused on sex due to deficits in other kinds of connection and because the intensity of sex *seems* like a quick and easy fix.[9]

Don't take this as suggestion that establishing emotional connections with one's own sex erases physical attraction—not at all! But when tempered by emotional satisfaction, sexual desire becomes less of a taskmaster and more of a lens to better understand and foster satisfying relationships. I used to want my attraction to men to go away—now, I see it as a gift that opens doors to deeply fulfilling relationships.

It's understandable if you're apprehensive about trying a new approach. Proceed with some caution, but definitely proceed. If you feel physical attraction to people of your sex, it's possible to vet people of your sex and determine who would be safe to share thoughts, feelings, or affection with without obscuring (via sex) real *relating*. It is also on you to establish and articulate healthful boundaries in *all* your relationships.[10]

Those who understand that emotional and social needs are legitimate, ongoing, and God-given grasp that meeting those needs healthfully rather than ignoring them can strengthen *all* relationships, even traditional marriage. Heck, it increases enjoyment of *every* good thing in life![11]

POINTS TO PONDER

- Nowhere in this book do I say that sex is inherently bad—nor do I say that gay sex fulfills or leads to lasting connection.
- God can help us fill needs—but He won't remove them. Same-sex *emotional* needs are God-given and *ongoing*. They must not be ignored. Why might God require us to work out our own solutions to meeting these needs?
- Emotional needs *can* appear as sexual desire, like feeling hungry when you're dehydrated. Can you think of habits or behaviors in your own life that aren't satisfying you in the ways you hope?
- Meeting emotional needs healthfully can illuminate true needs, open previously unimagined relational possibilities, and diminish selfish or unhealthful impulses toward others. It might also reduce compulsive behavior. What specific benefits have you seen when emotional needs are met?

NOTES

1. "No man is an island entire of itself. Every man is a piece of the continent, a part of the main." John Donne, *Devotions Upon Emergent Occasions* (London: Vintage, 1623) Ch. 17. See Jesse Johnson, "Why Men Need Other Men to Prosper," Vital Collective, n.d., https://vitalcollective.com/why-men-need-other-men-to-prosper/; Paul Friesen, "4 Things Men Need from Other Men (That They Can't Get from Women,"

Biola University Center for Marriage and Relationships, January 29, 2019, https://cmr.biola.edu/blog/2019/jan/29/4-things-men-need-other-men-they-cant-get-women/; Wednesday Lee Friday, "Women Are Often More Lonely Than We Let On," The Roots of Loneliness Project, 2022, accessed August 21, 2022, https://www.rootsofloneliness.com/lonely-women.

2. My sense is that the invention of the word *homosexual* has done severe damage to individuals and to society as a whole; it narrows all same-sex love down to one definition that denotes sexual expression. However, simple attraction to—a desire to be with—those of one's own sex has historically had an abundance of meanings and feelings for most people. Even when there has been intense love expressed between persons of the same sex, not all of them desired or expressed that love sexually. Most healthy people have some kind of attraction to their own sex, and these attractions have a variety of impetuses and manifestations. Linking sexual expression to the entire spectrum of same-sex attractions can cause bewilderment and self-doubt while also bringing outsider condemnation on "moral" grounds. See "How and When the Word Homosexual Was First Introduced into the Bible," Canyon Walker Connections (blog), November 25, 2017, https://canyonwalkerconnections.com/word-homosexual-first-introduced-bible/; Robert P. George, "The Philosophical Basis of Biblical Marriage," *Public Square Magazine*, January 6, 2022, https://publicsquaremag.org/faith/gospel-fare/the-philosophical-basis-of-biblical-marriage/.
3. Cultural norms can hold us back or inform us. I remember standing next to one of the "Lost Boys" (Sudanese refugee)

for some photographs to be taken; though we had barely met, he instinctively took my hand. Such behavior—including men kissing or walking arm in arm with men in some countries—has nothing to do with homosexuality but with natural affection. (A kiss between men in many cultures signifies neither an exclusive nor a sexual pairing.)

4. While important, fasting, prayer, scripture study—even willpower—were never enough to free me of compulsion, and nothing would take away my God-given need to connect healthfully with men.
5. Rather than take (or threaten to take) what brings an addict joy and connection, increase healthful versions of it! See American Addiction Institute, "Understanding the Root Cause of Addiction," American Institute of Mind and Medicine, 2020, https://american-addiction.com/lapse-vs-relapse/.
6. Kinsey Institute, "The Kinsey Scale," Indiana University, 2020, https://kinseyinstitute.org/research/publications/kinsey-scale.php. Newer, more detailed sexual orientation scales exist; this book uses Kinsey's for simplicity and familiarity. I acknowledge that even gender identity has complex biological and psychological nuances, but for simplicity in describing sexual orientation, I use basic male/female attractions here. Some people confuse same-sex attraction with pedophilia. I and most LGBTQIA and heterosexual people are not attracted to children. See Ian Johnston, "Pedophilia a 'Sexual Orientation—Like Being Straight or Gay,'" *Independent*, April 3, 2016, https://www.independent.co.uk/news/paedophilia-sexual-orientation-straight-gay-criminal-psychologist-child-sex-abuse-a6965956.html. Regarding options,

David A. Bednar says, "When we define ourselves by the labels of the world, we limit our divine potential and, in so doing, limit our ability to choose." "And Nothing Shall Offend Them," *Ensign*, November 2006, 89–92.

7. See chapter 10; Nazanin Moali, "Men, Arousal, and Erections: Why They Don't Always Come Together," Oasis2Care, last updated December 18, 2019, https://oasis2care.com/sexuality/men-arousal-and-erections-why-they-dont-always-come-together/; Go Ask Alice, "Can Erections Happen When You're Not Sexually Aroused," Columbia University, last updated April 30, 2015, https://goaskalice.columbia.edu/answered-questions/can-erections-happen-when-youre-not-sexually-aroused; McGill, "I May Have an Erection but I'm Just Not That Into It," *McGill University News and Events*, last updated July 23, 2013, https://www.mcgill.ca/channels/news/i-may-have-erection-i%E2%80%99m-just-not-it-229207; "Is an Erection Always an Indication of a Sexual Arousal or Attraction? Why or Why Not?" Quora, n.d., https://www.quora.com/Is-an-erection-always-an-indication-of-a-sexual-arousal-or-attraction-Why-or-why-not.
8. See Morton Hunt, "About Men; The Comfort of Pals," *The New York Times*, January 18, 1987, https://www.nytimes.com/1987/01/18/magazine/about-men-the-comfort-of-pals.html.
9. See Lewis, *The Four Loves*, 57–91.
10. I must state that, at least for an addict, no rule, no boundary—no risk of jail, HIV, death by a psychopath, public humiliation, family destruction, loss of employment and everything and everyone—is sufficient deterrent to acting out or "using." To quote the experts, addiction is "cunning,

baffling, and powerful." *Sexaholics Anonymous* ("White Book," Brentwood, TN: Sexaholics Anonymous, 1984), 2. It's no fiction that the astounding intellect of Dr. Arthur C. Doyle's fictional character Sherlock Holmes was no match against his own opioid addiction (you likely know real-life examples). How is it that I don't want my "drug of choice" today? Grace and the superior connections that actually meet my needs (see chapters 10–11).

11. See Chantelle Pattemore, "How to Set Boundaries in Your Relationships," Psych Central (blog), last updated June 3, 2021, https://psychcentral.com/blog/why-healthy-relationships-always-have-boundaries-how-to-set-boundaries-in-yours. On ongoing emotional need: "She does not realise that the husband whom she succeeds in isolating from his own kind will not be very well worth having." Lewis, *The Four Loves*, 15, 76. See also Matt Walsh, "The Most Effective Way to Destroy Your Husband, Ruin Your Marriage, and Encourage Infidelity," *The Daily Wire*, n.d., https://www.dailywire.com/news/walsh-most-effective-way-destroy-your-husband-ruin-matt-walsh.

CHAPTER 5

Freedom & Options—Beyond Either/Or

Why can't there be gay marriages in the Church of Jesus Christ? Are the only options for believing LGBTQIA people to let feelings override convictions or to live lonely?

YOU MAY OR MAY NOT HAVE doubts about God, but I hope you'll indulge me in answering the above questions (questions that you've likely asked yourself or others). They're more than just interesting points related to sexuality; these questions are crucial to getting the most out of relationships.

The benefits of premarital chastity and marital fidelity have been studied and documented significantly, mostly in heterosexual pairings.[1] Still, gay living doesn't cause unwanted pregnancies or create single parent homes (at least, not instantly). What possible harm can come from it? Do the disadvantages of premarital sexual activity and infidelity apply to gays? Why might God hold gays to the same chastity standards as heterosexual people?

In attempting to answer the above questions over the next few chapters, I share some concepts which have persuaded me that Christ's moral standards are not about inequity but about lasting joy for *everyone*. This point may seem like a tangent, but it is quite important to answering the enormous questions above. If a person rules out God as a rational belief, they can only view His standards as baseless and those who follow them as foolish. Additionally, ruling out God as a reasonable source of insight leaves people with incomplete information—and *fewer* options.

Two traditionally "Christian" ideas have caused countless people distress and alienation from God:

1. God invented justice (false)
2. God is omnipotent (true)

Some people feel Christianity lacks credibility, presuming that *both* of the above statements are doctrine. They ask (validly), "Why would an all-powerful God make laws and consequences, then send His Son to suffer consequences so we could get around the rules?"

To phrase it differently, "If God is omnipotent, why doesn't He just get rid of rules, consequences, and evil?

Is it possible that some things simply can't be eliminated? Unlike other Christians, members of The Church of Jesus Christ of Latter-day Saints believe that some things were not created but have always existed. These include the following:

- Intelligences (us)
- Matter
- Good and evil
- Agency (free will) and justice (consequence)

We are older than the stars! Creation *ex nihilo*—that is, from nothing—flies in the face of physical law. God is a being of reason and logic. The Hebrew word used for *create* in Genesis means "to organize."[2]

God not only organizes extant matter, but He also organized the hosts of heaven (us). Each of us is an *eternal* intelligence who (before coming to earth) was born voluntarily to heavenly parents into bodies of spirit, some male, some female. God is literally the "Father of [our] spirits."[3]

When we grasp that every one of us is (to modify Catholic phraseology) of the "same substance" as God—that the substance that makes up your spirit literally comes from God's very essence—we see that no one is a mere creation or product. In other words, you are not a building an architect designed; you are a child of the Architect—with the potential to grow to be like Him and enjoy all that He knows, all that He has, and all that He can do (with His blessing!). Ask a child, and he or she can tell you a calf doesn't grow to be a horse, but a cow or bull; a kitten becomes an adult cat; and a child of God can grow to be and "inherit all things." You belong! God's feelings for you are truly familial; we are *all* literally siblings, and your potential is unlimited.[4]

GOOD & EVIL

If you're unsure about the existence of good and evil, here's a simple definition: Good is voluntarily giving of self for the benefit of others; evil is putting personal gratification or gain above that of others. (Goodness doesn't ignore self-care, which everyone must do or die.) I'm not sure I've met anyone, atheist or believer, who hasn't found satisfaction in doing something kind for another person or emptiness in putting self before others or using them. These results are so consistent that we alter our behavior to avoid the emptiness of selfishness. One might loosely associate good and evil with yin and yang or with order and chaos.

While God isn't the author of evil, evil has always existed, and it affects us all. Some people, in their minds, still hold omnipotent God responsible for evil because He allows opposition (for His purposes).[5]

Because we are children of a benevolent God who loves us, I'm confident that we exist to attain joy—lasting, jump-up-and-down kind of joy.[6] Why would a loving parent allow painful things to happen to children He loves? That is a question worth pondering very carefully.[7]

AGENCY & JUSTICE

This concept is vital to understanding the character of God: Independent of God's judgment, independent of mortal courts, eternal justice exacts compensation for any and all loss or harm, whether or not harm was intended. There must be equilibrium, regardless of the cost of restoring that balance (recall science's universal law that every action has an "equal and opposite reaction"). Every choice has *always* been attached to a natural, equal and opposite, consequence. When we know that consequence is not a construct but occurs naturally; that each of us makes mistakes and breaks eternal laws with fixed consequences, the cost of which we cannot possibly pay; that we need a willing Redeemer—able to pay the price for us, then we can grasp that God did *not* send his Son to die to get around His own made-up demand for justice![8]

God is omnipotent because He knows all laws and is bound to follow them. He is one hundred percent true, sincere, and accurate; there is nothing mistaken, dishonest, or inequitable in Him.

If God didn't work within the parameters of justice and the eternal principle of action and reaction, He would not be God; matter would not conform to His will because He would be trying to make it behave contrary to the laws of physics or truth. He would not be omnipotent, and all would be chaos—because order comes from Him. We would likewise never benefit from the order God offers. Order is *highly* underrated! Law and order actually maximize freedom and options overall.[9]

An important aspect of God's omnipotence and order is that we have free will and that God honors it. Unlike matter, which always conforms to law, *intelligences* have agency—while subject to physical laws, we mostly do as we please; God knows that the only way for free agents to gain long-term happiness is to choose it freely. That is, we choose to act for good (or evil; free agents are not typically compelled or acted on).[10] God commands us, but He will not force us. (God has never forced me to pray—has He forced you?)[11] God will never cease to be God because He loves and lives according to law, and that eternal law includes allowing us our agency.

God's perfect plan for our happiness includes opportunities to learn how to use our agency wisely. Our mortal bodies are a priceless gift that we can use to learn discipline and self-control, including learning to control and channel our physical desires.

This life is a test, a chance for *us* to learn what we value above other options. During mortality, equity is scarce, and justice is often significantly delayed. In this test, we get some things wrong; just as moths are attracted both to food and to lethal flame, we are enticed by things that are good for us and by things that are bad for us—all with the intent that we learn to choose what brings long-term joy. In this fallen state, none of us is able to do good without help.[12] We learn essential lessons from our mistakes, but once we've broken even one eternal law, we are stranded outside God's perfect, happy presence, unfit to bear His brilliance and perfection.[13] How do we reconcile necessary eternal education with a now-unattainable goal?

Though He didn't invent justice, God *can* be credited for a spectacular innovation: mercy. God knew of a condition under which all of justice's demands could be met by one rare and specific kind of person, someone who had never broken a law and who could also endure all consequences without being extinguished. Jesus Christ's atoning sacrifice overcomes *all* obstacles to lasting joy—including broken laws (and bones and promises and homes).

Perfect Christ was able to pay for *all* broken laws because He never broke a law (was never obligated to justice) and His Father is immortal; as "God," Jesus could endure and absorb all consequences. Yet, as a mortal son of Mary, He could voluntarily suffer pain and death (the price required by justice for some actions).[14]

Christ's atoning sacrifice not only restores equilibrium to the universe by compensating for our errors; if we want, it also strengthens and perfects us. The benefits of Christ's atoning sacrifice are sometimes immediate and sometimes gradual, but they are sufficient to eventually make us flawless, if we want that. Having satisfied justice completely via His sufferings and death, Christ now holds the destinies of all acquitted offenders; that is, all of us.[15]

Like any loving parent, God doesn't want us staying home from school every day eating and viewing whatever we want, even if it's what would make us happy *now*. No parent wants their child miserable; most understand that the best and most lasting joys come by way of some struggle—even difficulty. Still, this life isn't meant to be all sacrifice for postponed rewards, neither is it all cartoons and Cocoa Puffs™ from birth until death; even as a test, life has both pain *and* happiness.

Opposition is good for us. Achieving any goal requires planning, work, learning new information or skills, sacrifice, and prioritization. Our greatest growth comes from work and from struggle; extract a butterfly from its cocoon and it will likely miss the individual exit labor needed to strengthen it for survival. It's not possible or even desirable to avoid all the pains of life, but by making wise choices, we can reduce suffering.

Our test isn't that we'll "be good" (which is impossible on our own) but that we'll choose Christ's goodness to be *our* goodness, to let His transformative power work with our sincere desires. If we can trust Christ, keep trying to turn from error, be baptized via His authority, and receive the gift of the Holy Spirit, we will live not only with God but also like Him.[16] These are Christ's requirements, and such steps are our choices rather than justice's dispassionate or lethal consequences. Choosing Christ and His path will bring joy plus "all that my Father hath" as "joint heirs with Christ." Technically, inheriting everything means we will inherit Christ's perfection, if we choose.[17]

By remembering our accountability for our own choices as well as God's sincere desire for our success and joy, we're less inclined to doubt or to ask, "Why me?" when we are in difficulty. Even death will not be a terror. There will always be opposition, and we'll have to struggle to gain insights, but we will have the perspective of our faith and, hopefully, a peace that transcends even in the worst circumstances of mortality.

Because we have a perfectly generous, loving Savior, our options are limitless. Because He can see everything at once, God is able to guide us, even in our mistakes, and turn our struggles into opportunities for growth and joy, even lasting joy. There are no dead ends or last chances if God, and sharing everything that is His, is our goal.[18]

POINTS TO PONDER

- We have always existed; agency and opposition have always existed. What would life be like without options and free will?
- God, our loving Heavenly Father, will not take our free will (though we can lose it to compulsions via poor choices). Likewise, consequences for choices are not a construct that God can waive (or wave away). How do you reconcile God's love for us and His respect for both free will and natural consequences?
- Everything God does is to *maximize* our freedom and happiness. How does this idea affect your perception of God or of your choices and your situation?

NOTES

1. Nathaniel M. Lambert and David C. Dollahite, "Forsaking All Others: Marital Fidelity in Religious Couples," *BYU Journal of Undergraduate Research* (September 2013), http://jur.byu.edu/?p=6130. See also Matthew D. Bramlett and

Laura F. Radel, "Adverse Family Experiences among Children in Nonparental Care, 2011–2012," *National Health Statistics Reports* 74 (May 2014), https://www.cdc.gov/nchs/data/nhsr/nhsr074.pdf; Paul Amato, "The Impact of Family Formation Change on the Cognitive, Social, and Emotional Well-Being of the Next Generation," *The Future of Children*, Volume 15, Number 2, (Fall 2005): 75–96, https://muse.jhu.edu/article/188645; Marissa A. Fye and Grace A. Mims, "Preventing Infidelity: A Theory of Protective Factors," *The Family Journal* 27, no. 1 (January 2019), 22–30, https://doi.org/10.1177/1066480718809428; Marvin Daguplo, "Marital Fidelity," ResearchGate, January 2017, https://www.researchgate.net/publication/312460727_Marital_Fidelity; Mallory Mosner, "Why I'm Breaking Up with Non-Monogamy," Medium (blog), February 3, 2020, https://mmosner.medium.com/why-im-breaking-up-with-non-monogamy-324c393c6d03.

2. "Creation from Chaos," Pearl of Great Price Central, Last modified November 12, 2019, https://www.pearlofgreatpricecentral.org/creation-from-chaos/. See https://PremioBooks.com/joy for expanded notes and active links.
3. "Moses [said]: 'When the most High . . . separated the sons of Adam, he set the bounds of the people . . .' (Deut. 32:8), this is a . . . reference to *pre-earth* assignments. . . . The Septuagint has a variant reading . . . 'sons of God,' from fragments of Deuteronomy 32 discovered in cave 4 of Qumran sustain . . . 'ben Elohim.'" Joseph F. McConkie, "Premortal Existence, Foreordinations, and Heavenly Councils" in *Apocryphal Writings and the Latter-day Saints*, ed. C. Wilfred Griggs (West Valley City: Bookcraft, 1986),

https://rsc.byu.edu/apocryphal-writings-latter-day-saints/premortal-existence-foreordinations-heavenly-councils; Stephen O. Smoot, "The Divine Council in the Hebrew Bible and the Book of Mormon," *Studia Antiqua* 12, no. 2 (2013): 1–18, https://archive.bookofmormoncentral.org/content/divine-council-hebrew-bible-and-book-mormon. See also Bokovoy, "Ye Really Are Gods," A Response to Michael Heiser Concerning the LDS Use of Psalm 82 and the Gospel of John," *Review of Books on the Book of Mormon 1989–2011* 19, no. 1 (2007), https://scholarsarchive.byu.edu/cgi/viewcontent.cgi?article=1702&context=msr; Num. 16:22; Deut. 14:1; Job 38:4–7; Ps. 82:6; Eccl. 12:7; Jer. 1:4–5; Hosea 1:10; Mal. 2:10; John 9:2; Acts 17:28–29; Rom. 8:16, 29; 1 Cor. 11:7; 2 Thess. 2:13; Heb. 12:9; Jude 1:6; Rev. 10, 5:3, 12:7–11, 13:8; Alma 13:3; Hel. 14:17; D&C 38:1, 49:17, 93:23–38, 138:53–56; Moses 3:5, 6:51; Abr. 3:21–26; LDS Topical Guide, "Beginning," "Council in Heaven," "Man, Men," "War in Heaven."

4. Omniscience does not equate to adoration. I believe that *only* the Godhead (Father, Son, Holy Spirit) will be worshipped in eternity. We may attain perfection, but man is not the Architect or Atoning Hero or Sanctifier of humanity. 2 Pet. 1:4; Gen. 17:1; Matt. 5:48; John 3:2, 10:32–34, 17:22–23. See also Boyd K. Packer, *Let Not Your Heart Be Troubled* (Salt Lake City: Bookcraft, 1991), 289; C. S. Lewis, "Counting the Cost" in *Mere Christianity* (New York: Harper One, 2015); C. S. Lewis, "Love Thy Neighbor" in *The Joyful Christian* (New York: Scribner, 1996).
5. While John Calvin gave us valuable insights, he also introduced serious problems into modern Christian theology:

Because John Calvin did not believe in a premortal existence, he assumed that God created people at the time of their mortal birth. That assumption presented . . . a theological dilemma: . . . (1) God is perfect, therefore his creations are . . . perfect; (2) However, some of his creations are bad and are going to go to hell; (3) Therefore, either God messed up when he created them (not an acceptable conclusion), or he did not err; (4) If he did not err, then he created them exactly the way he wanted them to be; (5) Therefore, he created the bad people with the intent that they should go to hell; (6) Conclusion: God created some people to go to heaven, and other people to go to hell. That [erroneous idea] is called predestination. Stephen D. Ricks and LeGrand L. Baker, *Alma 14: The Origins of Good & Evil* (Salt Lake City: Eborn Books, 2011), 586–606, https://archive.bookofmormoncentral.org/sites/default/files/archive-files/pdf/baker/2015-12-30/baker_alma_14_2011.pdf.

"How can a God intent on saving His children and desirous to 'wipe away all tears from their eyes' (Rev. 21:4) also damn them to eternal punishment?" Garrett R. Maxwell, "The Good God Hermeneutic: A Reconsideration of Religious Vocabulary," *Interpreter: A Journal of Latter-day Saint Faith and Scholarship* 47 (2021), 151–58, https://archive.bookofmormoncentral.org/content/good-god-hermeneutic-reconsideration-religious-vocabulary. Instances where the Bible indicates that God caused evil or temptation or hardened someone's heart are mistranslations. See also https://PremioBooks.com/joy.

6. 2 Ne. 2:25.
7. 2 Ne. 2:11.
8. God didn't invent justice, but God is just. Alma 42:13. See "Newton's Laws of Motion," Glenn Research Center, last updated June 30, 2022, https://www1.grc.nasa.gov/beginners-guide-to-aeronautics/newtons-laws-of-motion/; H. Donl Peterson, "The Law of Justice and the Law of Mercy" in *The Book of Mormon: Alma, the Testimony of the Word*, ed. Monte S. Nyman and Charles D. Tate Jr. (Provo, UT: Religious Studies Center, Brigham Young University, 1992), 211–22, https://rsc.byu.edu/book-mormon-alma-testimony-word/law-justice-law-mercy.
9. See Harrison P. Frye, "Freedom without Law," *Politics, Philosophy & Economics* 17, no. 3 (August 2018), 298–316, https://doi.org/10.1177/1470594X17742746; "How Does the Rule of Law Promote Freedom?" Brainly question, August 12, 2020, https://brainly.in/question/30559573; and John A. Bruegger, "Freedom, Legality, and the Rule of Law," *Washington University Jurisprudence Review* 9, no. 1 (2016), https://openscholarship.wustl.edu/cgi/viewcontent.cgi?article=1151&context=law_jurisprudence.
10. 2 Ne. 2:14, 25; Jac. 4:6. See W. Cleon Skousen, "The Atonement," Spiritual Thoughts and Genealogy, n.d., https://www.emogan.com/blog/spiritual-thoughts/atonement-cleon-skouson.
11. God did not force us to be born on earth (many of His spirit children chose *not* to receive physical bodies). God's plan of happiness requires opposition and options from which to choose. Gen. 2:16; Josh. 24:15. Yet, our first parents had to voluntarily choose opposition; choice was always the

plan, and only possible in temporal bodies with minds that understood right and wrong. The tree of knowledge facilitated that—that is why God included it in the garden. Christ was never the backup plan; He is the Lamb *already* "slain from before the foundation of the world." Rev. 13:8; Isa. 53:4; 2 Ne. 31; Alma 7:11–12.

Our coming into [earth] would have been counterproductive if a way had not been provided for us to . . . return home in . . . cognizance . . . so we could escape . . . greater chaos—the natural consequence of mortal sin . . . death and hell. . . . [Prophets] explained, . . . "God, commanded. . . of the tree of the knowledge of good and evil, thou shalt not eat . . . nevertheless, thou mayest choose." . . . The laws of justice and mercy insist that [God not proclaim free access. Had] God . . . [told] them to eat that fruit . . . *He* would have been responsible for their expulsion from the Garden [our separation from Him] and . . . for getting us back. That would have left us without . . . agency . . . or . . . freedom. . . . We . . . [left] the premortal spirit world . . . because we understood [God's] plan and trusted in the Savior's Atonement. We . . . chose to come. . . . Ricks and Baker, *Alma 14.*

Ricks and Baker say that, while "In the day thou eatest thereof thou shalt surely die," is often understood as a curse, it's actually one of the greatest promises God has given. He basically told our first parents, 'if you choose to exercise full agency like me—really experience good and evil in that lone and dreary world—I promise to let you eventually leave it via death; and I promise to send a Savior to overcome death and sin so that, once you have learned what you need to learn, you may return to live with me again. Alma 42:8-10. There would be no free will if everyone automatically returned to live with God without *choosing* Christ's rescue. Ricks and Baker, *Alma 14*.

12. Gen. 3:22; Job 1:12, 2:6, 7:18, 36:11; 2 Cor. 8:2; 1 Pet. 1:6; Abr. 3:25; Moses 4:28; 2 Ne. 9:27, 33:9; Alma 12:24, 42:4.
13. Thomas Edison gave details about what happens to matter that is unsuitable to bear pure light. See "Edison's Lightbulb," The Franklin Institute, n.d., https://www.fi.edu/history-resources/edisons-lightbulb; D&C 133:41.
14. Heb. 12:2; Moro. 10:32. See also Brad Wilcox, *The Continuous Atonement* (Salt Lake City: Deseret Book, 2009) for more on satisfying justice.
15. "He that believeth and is baptized shall be saved." Mark 16:16. "Believeth" implies ongoing belief. "Saved" means *in* God's presence. Joseph Smith, "The Articles of Faith" in the Pearl of Great Price (Salt Lake City: The Church of Jesus Christ of Latter-day Saints, 1902) 60; 2 Ne. 31:17–21.
16. Rev. 21:7. "Joint heirs" enjoy all blessings the Father has. See Luke 12:44, 15:31–32; Rom. 8:16–17; 1 Cor. 2:9, 3:21–23; D&C 84:38, 78:5–7, 132:20. See also David E. Bokovoy, "Ye Really *Are* Gods."
17. Matt. 5:48. "However late you think you are, however many chances you think you have missed, however many mistakes you feel you have made or talents you think you don't have, or however far from home and family and God you feel you have traveled, I testify that you have not traveled beyond the reach of divine love. It is not possible for you to sink lower than the infinite light of Christ's Atonement shines." Jeffrey R. Holland, "The Laborers in

the Vineyard," *Ensign*, May 2012, https://www.churchofjesuschrist.org/study/general-conference/2012/04/the-laborers-in-the-vineyard?lang=eng.

18. I obtained these insights by studying, pondering, and praying about the words of past and living prophets and the confirming impressions of the Holy Spirit—seeking corroboration in the scriptures. My faith doesn't ask me to accept mysteries but to seek answers. If you find the scriptures or spiritual concepts difficult to digest or believe, consider experimenting on God's promise in James 1:5–6: "If any of you lack wisdom, let him ask of God, that giveth to all men liberally, and upbraideth not; and it shall be given him. But let him ask in faith . . ." (See also Russell M. Nelson, "Revelation for the Church, Revelation for Our Lives," *Liahona*, May 2018, https://www.churchofjesuschrist.org/study/liahona/2018/05/sunday-morning-session/revelation-for-the-church-revelation-for-our-lives?lang=eng; Num. 11:29; Joel 2:28–29.) Additionally, acting on truth confirms personal conviction. See Amos 3:7; Matt. 7:16; John 7:17; Eph. 4:11–16.

CHAPTER 6

Is Fluidity Real?—Are Feelings Eternal?

Some choices are binary, with only two options: breathe or suffocate, eat or starve, sleep or try to stay awake. But most choices present multiple options; we are only limited in our choices by our ability to see alternatives. For a very long time, I could only see "limited" options!

BY PRESENTING MULTIPLE PATHS, I DON'T mean to imply that each is equally desirable—or that all paths are harmless. The natural consequences of what we choose can limit us physically or materially or spiritually; for example, people aware of our poor choices are less likely to trust us with things or opportunities, and we can even lose our liberty via incarceration or to chemical dependence or other addictions. Poor choices often reduce future choices.

I have known my share of addicts. What surprises me is how often *nonaddicts* express doubt about a loss of free will in addiction. Whether a physiological process actually retards cognitive ability or whether addiction can only be described as spiritual chains, I know that at one point in my life, I personally experienced a significant reduction in my ability to choose actions against feeding my compulsion. One person's ability to "control" their own appetite for alcohol (or food or drugs or sex) doesn't mean that another person has the same ability—or that the first person will always be able to maintain that level of control.[1]

When you've limited your options through poor choices, moving forward is like trying to climb out of a hole with inadequate tools: It's slow at best. For me, there was no instant fix to compulsive behavior. Transformative grace is often gradual. Some mistakenly assume that grace means God does it all. While I acknowledge that all metamorphic power is Christ's, I still bear the responsibility of studying my situation and discovering, with God's help, who I am and what is best for me. Then, I sincerely follow the "steps" we've established, and my action manifests that I want Christ's power to fill my deficits and help me reach my objectives.

The twelve steps of Alcoholics Anonymous have been invaluable in helping me come to Christ and receive power I did not have. That power, of course, is Christ's grace. I am talking here about power over compulsive behavior—not same-sex attraction. I am grateful for the gift of same-sex attraction. (There is something more powerful than the twelve steps for anything you face, which I'll share in another chapter.)

As I shared my feelings, thoughts, and deeds with other people, my compulsive sexual activity diminished. It was possible to actually say no. My social interactions became more nurturing. Interestingly, my own efforts weren't making these changes; I had tried willpower and anything else I could think of, but I had been unsuccessful. Instead, my steps were a mere demonstration that I sincerely wanted Christ's liberating grace, and it was given to me.

Sometimes I thought I was cured of my compulsions, and I'd stop working the twelve steps, slacking off on calling and meeting group members, only to relapse.[2] Part of my path includes rules to help me avoid relapse, because I know I'm not smarter than my addiction. Some of my early rules were unrealistic; for example, I forbid myself from being alone with another man with same-sex attraction (as if that were a detail I'd always know!). It wasn't that I didn't trust them; I didn't trust me.

Though shortsighted and sometimes hurtful to others, these rules were all I could come up with at the time. I believe God understood my intent and helped me, even in my ignorance. What I really needed was *increased* interaction with men who were unafraid of real connection, but at the time, I couldn't see many ways for that to happen, considering my compulsive history.

Of note, while I'd come very close to marrying women on multiple occasions, I never approached marriage with the idea that marriage would "fix" my sexual orientation. Because my attraction to men and women has ebbed and flowed, my expectation has mostly been that I'll one day be happily married to a woman (in this life or the next) while maintaining profound, affectionate relationships with men and women forever. I don't think I have seriously entertained, at least not as a mature adult, the idea that I would, in this life, "change" to a heterosexual. That is, I haven't viewed marriage to a woman as a "cure" for my same-sex attraction.

Still, we can imagine how disillusioned, discouraged, and even angry a person might feel if they were persuaded, by self or another person, that physical attraction to one's sex vanishes in mortality, only to fall maddeningly short of that goal or believe they'd achieved it and then "relapse." I can't judge anyone or their desires, but I wouldn't condone promising someone that it's likely they'll become heterosexual in this life. That said, I can see how someone who has experienced an ebb and flow of attraction for same and opposite sex, as I have, might persuasively tell themselves, "I am now heterosexual." I suspect it's more likely that they currently feel more heterosexual than gay. Some queer people never experience this, but fluidity in attraction is not unusual.[3]

IS *CHANGE* AN OFFENSIVE WORD?

Though not alcoholic, I've been in Alcoholics Anonymous meetings, and I know how maddening it might be for the usual addict to hear someone say, "One day, God took away my desire to drink, and I've never wanted a drop since." Yet, this sometimes is heard in AA meetings, and I believe people have experienced this (if only for people to see that God has all power).

Because of this phenomenon—and because I know God is a god of miracles—I won't rule out that God *could* take a willing same-sex attracted person and grant them complete satisfaction in heterosexual life *if* God had a purpose behind it. However, my sense is that most of us who are attracted to our own sex have a divine objective behind what we feel, and we will likely remain so attracted, at minimum while in mortality, to fulfill all the wonderful things associated with those feelings.

As for the durability of sexual orientation, I will not be so presumptuous as to declare without a doubt that same-sex physical attraction will never exist (at least temporarily) in the next life. You and I should be just as cautious about saying that it most definitely will exist for *all* eternity.[4] My own experience is that whom one is attracted to *can* be fluid, though it's important to remember that physical attraction alone is a poor basis for any relationship.[5]

WILL THERE BE HETEROSEXUALS IN HEAVEN?

I've had an illuminating epiphany: I used to think I had to become heterosexual *and then* become like Christ to live with God; now, I know that I only must become like Christ.

This concept of transformation, or "conversion" (spiritual, not sexual orientation), is central to God's plan for our happiness. Any heterosexual person who thinks a gay person must change if they want to live with God is right—and any gay person who thinks a heterosexual person must change to be saved is just as correct! We all have changes to make, but with grace, we all have hope. Why would God command that we become like Him if there is no way to do so?[6]

The responsibility to choose Christ is ours alone—the power to follow Him is not ours (more on this coming up). Prophets have written that God can change our very nature, but *never* against our will. God can eventually change us from whatever we are to be like Him. Each of us needs His character traits (while retaining what makes us individuals).[7]

Recall that those who seek to follow God are promised "all that my Father hath" as "joint heirs with Christ."[8] "Eye hath not seen, nor ear heard—neither have entered into the heart of [mortals] the things which God hath prepared for them that love him."[9] These things aren't just material; Christ can bestow on any willing person His very qualities—His very perfection.

Not only will everyone resurrect with flawless, immortal bodies after death, but also, I assume we will be the gender that we were before this life. Just as our mortal body allows us to experience sensations and joy, the perfect body we'll each be restored to is critical to experiencing bliss in eternity.[10] I believe that everyone will be ecstatic with their gender and all relationships in eternity. Gender is an eternal characteristic, or why should the eternal God of the universe ask us to call him Father?

Just as a follower of Christ with too strong a desire for treats (or for someone who is not available to them, regardless of gender) will, at some point in eternity, become a "new creature," perfect in Christ, I believe disciples who desire nuclear relationships with spouse and children in the next life will have and enjoy those things.[11] Considering how little we know about the life to come, it's presumptuous to think we know how anyone will feel being with the opposite sex.

Personally, I don't believe our need to foster relationships with those of our *own* sex will ever disappear, nor do I believe people will eternally want sexual relationships with their sex, just as I don't believe I will always want to eat donuts by the dozen in one sitting as I sometimes want to now.[12] I don't mean to say there is no pleasure in the next life, only that in God's kingdom, each of us will enjoy our perfect amount of cinnamon or hugs or magenta that most pleases us individually. My views aren't solely a result of my experience with fluidity but are also products of reason and precedent with grace: I've experienced significant changes already going from entrenched sex addiction to more healthful relating with both sexes.

Whether it is by a change in us and our desires or by receiving something better than we *ever* hoped for, no one in God's kingdom will feel denied, cheated of, or lacking anything. I know God loves us *all*.[13]

POINTS TO PONDER

- As you read, you may see that your journey, or your loved one's, is similar to mine. You'll also see some differences, maybe significant ones. What can you learn from the similarities and differences in our experiences?
- By presenting multiple paths, I don't mean to imply that each is equally desirable—or that all are harmless. How have your choices taught you this?
- When I speak of God's love for and acceptance of queer persons, I'm not saying it's merely tolerance—neither am I saying it's acceptance of gay sex as a positive expression of gayness. God not only accepts queerness, but it is part of His plan for mortal happiness. How does our diversity serve God's purposes and our happiness?
- People attracted to their own sex will likely remain so attracted, at least while in mortality, for wonderful purposes. I believe everyone will be ecstatic with their gender in eternity and that all relationships will be beyond satisfying—and we needn't wait until then. Whether it is by a change in us or our desires or by receiving something better than we ever hoped for, no one in God's kingdom will feel denied, cheated of, or lacking anything (Ps. 23:5). What insights do you gain by viewing gender and sexuality with an eternal perspective?

NOTES

1. See Denise Cummins, "The Myth and Reality of Free Will: The Case of Addiction," Psychology Today (blog), February 9, 2014, https://www.psychologytoday.com/us/blog/good-thinking/201402/the-myth-and-reality-free-will-the-case-addiction.
2. I was never addicted to alcohol, but when I first moved to Utah, I had trouble locating a twelve-step meeting for sex addicts, so I attended AA. (My responses to inquiries about my "drug of choice" were entertaining!)
3. "What Does Sexually Fluid Mean?" Web MD, November 27, 2021, https://www.webmd.com/sex-relationships/what-does-sexually-fluid-mean. See also "Can Sexuality Change? What Sexual Fluidity Is and Is Not," Good Therapy (blog), June 24, 2018, https://www.goodtherapy.org/blog/can-sexuality-change-what-sexual-fluidity-is-and-is-not-0624187/amp/.
4. Some cite the ancient American leader Alma: The "same spirit which doth possess your bodies at the time that ye go out of this life . . . will have power to possess your body in that eternal world." Alma 34:34. Yet, this passage doesn't say "eternally" (it says "in that eternal world")—the next *sphere* is eternal, not a sprit's hold on a person! (See D&C 19.) My experience with fluid attraction informs me that people are creatures of change—especially when God is involved—though no change will be forced on anyone. As a side note, over my lifetime, my attraction to women and men has evolved in satisfying ways.
5. (I think people's grasp of some fluidity in their own lives is at the heart of much homophobia.) Evaluate your own

changes—and those of people you know. While you personally may never have experienced changes in attraction, you likely know someone like me—and you likely have experienced other kinds of changes. What do Christians believe about change? Will a person *eternally* want to be with someone else's spouse? I used to hate pumpkin pie; I *love* it now! I used to love board games; not much now. I thought I didn't like sci-fi movies—then I saw *Star Wars*. As a young man, I believed I could never be a physical threat to anyone; but just observe me if someone puts my loved ones in peril. We are all on a spectrum, a continuum of metamorphoses. No one is static or cemented into a slot. As children of God, we've already gone from eternal intelligences to having spirit bodies to having physical bodies, and we will change again—back to spirit bodies (at death), then with a physical body again, only perfected. See 1 Cor. 15:40; 2 Cor. 12:2; D&C 76, 93:33–37; Alma 34.

6. Matt. 5:48. Martin Luther King Jr. famously said, "People fail to get along because they fear each other; they fear each other because they don't know each other; they don't know each other because they have not communicated with each other." Understanding one's self (and God) well can also eliminate much fear. "Referring to our brothers and sisters in a way that conveys disbelief in their capacity to change would also convey disbelief in the power of the Savior and His Atonement." Joni L. Koch, "To Be or Have Been; That Is the Question," *Ensign*, October 2019, 52.
7. "God is the author of diversity and the source of unity. As we come closer to Him and to His Son, Jesus Christ, we will

advance both powerful principles in a synergistic way. As we embrace our true primary identity as children of God and act as disciples of Christ, they will magnify our individual gifts while also making us more united." Kevin J. Worthen, "Persevere in Unity," BYU devotional, January 12, 2021, https://speeches.byu.edu/talks/kevin-j-worthen/unity/. See also 2 Cor. 5:17.

8. Rom. 8:16–17, Matt. 5:48.
9. "Joint heirs" enjoy all blessings the Father has. See Luke 12:44, 15:31–32; 1 Cor. 2:9, 3:21–23; Rev. 21:7; D&C 84:38, 78:5–7, 132:20.
10. Note the denotation (direct implications) of the word *restoration* in Acts 3:19–21 and Alma 40 and 41. See "The Family: A Proclamation to the World," The Church of Jesus Christ of Latter-day Saints, accessed February 18, 2022, https://www.churchofjesuschrist.org/study/scriptures/the-family-a-proclamation-to-the-world/the-family-a-proclamation-to-the-world?lang=eng.
11. Gen. 2:18, 2:24, 22:17, 25:8, 32:12, 35:29, 49:33; Exod. 32:13; Eccl. 3:14; Isa. 51:2, 65:23; Jer. 31:1; Mal. 4:6; Matt. 16:19, 18:18, 19:5, 19:8, 19:29; Mark 10:9, 10:30; 1 Cor. 2:9, 11:11; 2 Cor. 5:17; Eph. 3:14–15, 5:31; 1 Pet. 3:7; Moses 3:18, 3:24, 7:63; Abr. 5:18; 3 Ne. 25:6; D&C 131:2, 132:19, 132:55. "And that same sociality which exists among us here will exist among us [in heaven], only it will be coupled with eternal glory," D&C 130:2. Perhaps you feel left out not being married; you're certainly not alone. Still, the same prophets that have taught the benefits of eternal marriages have also taught that vicariously performed sacraments/ordinances, like marriage, are

available to anyone in the next life who desires them and whose current quest is to keep covenants—not that spirits of the dead or resurrected people are "given in marriage" in the next life. Marriage, and other ordinances/sacraments, can only be performed by those with mortal bodies, but they can be done vicariously by mortals, to be accepted or rejected by the dead (like Christ's vicarious sacrifice). See Mark 10:30; 1 Cor. 15:29; Heb. 10:12; 1 Pet. 2:24–25; 1 John 2:12, 4:10. None of this means we won't enjoy eternal relationships with people of our own sex. Those who keep covenants with God will not be denied any blessing. See "Church Policies & Guidelines," *General Handbook: Serving in The Church of Jesus Christ of Latter-day Saints* 38.1.4, accessed February 14, 2022, https://www.churchofjesuschrist.org/study/manual/general-handbook/38-church-policies-and-guidelines?lang=eng. See also "The Family: A Proclamation to the World."

12. Ps. 23:5; Jer. 31:14; 1 Cor. 2:9; D&C 84:38, 78:5–7, 132:20. See also Luke 12:44, 15:31–32; Rev. 21:7.
13. I don't believe it's healthful to hide one's feelings, nor do I believe that becoming heterosexual is likely in this life. When I speak of God's love for and acceptance of queer persons, I'm *not* saying it's merely tolerance—neither am I saying it's acceptance of gay sex as a positive expression of gayness.

CHAPTER 7

Is Mixed-Orientation Marriage a Happy Option for Some Attracted to Their Own Sex?

"Well, actually, I didn't choose who I fell in love with. It just happened. I am attracted to men, and [to my wife] Susan."[1]

—*Brett Croche*

SOME MEMBERS OF MY CHURCH ERRONEOUSLY think they have to be married to dwell with God. Not only will God never force you to marry someone you don't want to marry, but also, He will never force you to marry *anyone.* (Still, keep your options open! See chapter 13.) If we remember who He is and what He's about, we will have no apprehension.[2]

As I've already shared, I sought marriage to different women multiple times for a number of positive reasons. When my relationships with women ended—breakups were about evenly split between me calling it off and the ladies doing so—it was rarely because of my attraction to men. I typically didn't share that aspect of my life unless we were seriously contemplating marriage. However, when I disclosed my orientation to the girl I most wanted to marry, she dumped me—adding that she wouldn't recommend me to any woman. That was quite a blow. It's important to note that not all women responded this way when I shared this vital part of who I am.

Many people who are attracted to their own sex have never acted on those feelings. Some married someone of the opposite sex and had families; some wanted to, and others felt led to marriage by the Holy Spirit. Those who argue that a mixed-orientation marriage (gay/bi man with a heterosexual woman or lesbian/bi woman with a heterosexual man) cheats the nongay spouse might not be acknowledging that person's agency and ability to reason, so long as the gay spouse disclosed their sexual orientation when contemplating marriage. Importantly, I've known mixed-orientation couples who are adamant that God led them to marry. Some men found no women attractive *except* for the one they married.

Some in mixed-orientation marriages felt pressured to marry by family or by church leaders. Some naively believed that marriage would "resolve" or "cure" same-sex attraction; if anyone was counseled by a leader that this would be the outcome, that is grievous, yet Christ's atoning sacrifice can compensate us for every suffering or loss.[3]

God's earthly kingdom has never been led by perfect people: Moses killed a man, and Peter denied the Christ.[4] Though there's an unfortunate history of well-meaning but misguided leaders giving bad instruction in counseling their same-sex–attracted parishioners, today, no faithfully informed Church of Jesus Christ leader counsels people to marry as a means of managing or eliminating same-sex attraction.[5]

Mixed-orientation marriages are complicated, but even those that end can bring blessings. Interestingly, the gay parents I know don't regret having had children in mixed-orientation marriages. On the contrary, they say their children (and other things) made marriage worth any effort or sacrifice—even if they later divorced. It's notable that some of these people were promised by clergy that they would be blessed if they married (despite same-sex attraction) and that these parents are quick to say that their children are the greatest blessing of their lives.

Many people in mixed-orientation marriages are content where they are, and I suspect these couples are vastly undercounted. They have weighed the pros and cons and have decided they prefer the cooperative roles and blessings that "traditional" union offers. We don't hear about these couples much because they don't typically broadcast their status or their experiences. Some people argue that such people are in denial or are controlled by religion. The reality is that while some young adults might be in denial about personal attractions, most adults come to be pretty certain about feelings in that area and have based their relationships on deliberate decisions.

By contrast, some same-sex–attracted people are not content in mixed-orientation marriage and feel they are living a lie. Some become overwhelmed by the real and legitimate need to connect with those of their own sex in some way because that particular social and emotional need is not met by an opposite-sex spouse.

Whatever your past or current domestic situation, I hope that my experience may inform your journey toward fulfillment and spare you or someone you love worse pain than what you or they might currently know. I am *not* about to propose that you bottle up your feelings or deny your true self. There are happy options beyond the closet, potentially isolating marriages, or a worldly gay social scene.

Some married people secretly hook up sexually with people of their sex. Some declare their situation to their spouses and divorce; others declare their feelings and work to stay married. I have met a great many people in a variety of situations. Those who embrace gay sex believe that this new way of life is the honest, authentic way to be—free from restrictions. Others begin a disciplined, but disappointing, quest for one person who will meet *all* their same-sex partner expectations.

Some seeking a same-sex partner are unpleasantly surprised to find that gays are imperfect too, full of all the same flaws, vices, and annoying quirks an opposite-sex partner might have. In my experience—speaking generally—gay men are more fickle than the many strong and beautiful women I've known who incline toward fidelity. I believe there are fundamental reasons for this (and will address them shortly).

Even in functional mixed-orientation marriages, trust can be an ongoing issue. Some of my gay and bi guy friends who are married to women are in situations where, regardless of fidelity to their wives, they are required to account to their wives 24/7 as to their whereabouts. Heaven forbid any of them should be delayed! One friend in particular is afraid he won't have access to his grandchildren if his wife decides she doesn't want him around anymore, so he submits to her perpetual accounting of his whereabouts.

What if the shoe is on the other foot, and you're the opposite-sex spouse? Are you afraid your same-sex–attracted spouse might get sexual with a gay person? Are you willing to trust your spouse in close, emotionally bonded relationships with their same-sex friends? Do you encourage those relationships and the time spent on them? Sexual infidelity is more likely to happen when God-given social and emotional needs *aren't* met healthfully.

Consider that no one person can meet all of another's needs, even among spouses. Your spouse's healthy same-sex relationships (and yours!) won't erode your marriage but will strengthen it by adding to your individual wholeness. Consider that your spouse may be unable to find a heterosexual person who will share the weight of their unique struggles through talk, touch, and comfort; they might *only* find a gay same-sex friend willing to do that. Yes, there is a risk of sex, but it's comparable to the infidelity risk of a heterosexual marriage; has any spouse, in all of history, been free of the risk of being cheated on? Putting our loved ones in God's hands can significantly reduce anxiety and pain. Not only can God help people do what they couldn't do alone, but He can also help each of us past legitimate and irrational fear. It's what He does. He loves us all.[6]

God knows, perfectly, that our greatest joys come from relationships. Still, long-term bliss with a *partner* is elusive, even for heterosexual people. God is needed in all our relating—though true fulfillment may not look like what we currently are told or imagine it to be.[7]

Relationships between people of the same sex can be among the most profound and rewarding, but they manifest distinctly from what the world tells us to expect. Consider King David and Jonathan's strong union (though every indication conveys that they each loved women deeply).[8] Jesus had a supernal connection with John the Beloved.[9] Many Apostles have used expressions such as "indescribable bond" when speaking of their love for one another. I've had a heterosexual church leader affirm to me that while he loves his wife dearly, his love for his two male church assistants is exquisite.[10]

Same-sex relationships can create bonds that can last forever if the participants are true to the unique, God-given expression of such love. The simplistic partnering stories the world tells to and about gays can create agonizingly destructive expectations, though it's worth noting that "romanticism" creates impossible expectations for people of all orientations. All the same, there is more than hope for happy same-sex relationships for those willing to scrutinize and perhaps adjust what they currently believe leads to lasting fulfillment. I'm not speaking of learning to live with the next best thing—nor with sexual infidelity—but of a path to lasting fulfillment and intimacy.[11]

POINTS TO PONDER

- Awareness of options empowers us and increases our chances for fulfillment. There are happier options than what the world highlights for us: the closet, potentially isolating marriages, or a sexualized gay scene—better choices for relating to one another. What might other options look like for you or your loved one?
- Most LGBTQIA parents count their children among their greatest blessings. In what ways have you been blessed while still struggling to find God's path for you?
- Whether gay, heterosexual, or mixed-orientation, we need God's help to find the bliss we hope for

from our relationships. Same-sex relationships *can* involve profound bonding that can, with care, last forever. How can you include God in your relationships as you build and maintain them?

NOTES

1. Brett Croche (personal social media post, 2022).
2. Mark 16:16; Ether 5:5. While faithful covenant marriage between a man and a woman might be necessary to have offspring in eternity, it has never been a requirement to live happily with God. Any person who follows Christ once they learn of His plan, and for whom a temple marriage was not feasible in this life, will have the option to receive eternal marriage and posterity—if they want those blessings. Spirits of the dead or resurrected people are *not* "given in marriage" in the next life; marriage and other ordinances/sacraments, like baptism, can only be performed by those with mortal bodies, but they can be done vicariously by mortals, to be accepted or rejected by the dead (as Christ's atoning sacrifice was vicariously done for living and dead while He was in His mortal body). See 1 Cor. 15:29; Heb. 10:12; 1 Pet. 2:24–25; 1 John 2:12, 4:10. See also D&C 131, 132; D. Todd Christofferson, "Why Marriage, Why Family," *Ensign*, May 2015, 50–53.
3. "All your losses will be made up to you in the resurrection, provided you continue faithful." Joseph Smith Jr., *Teachings of the Prophet Joseph Smith*, comp. Joseph F. Smith (Salt Lake City: Deseret Book, 1977), 84. "All that is unfair about life can be made right through the Atonement of Jesus Christ."

"Lesson 2: The Plan of Salvation" in *Preach My Gospel: A Guide to Missionary Service* (Salt Lake City: The Church of Jesus Christ of Latter-day Saints, 2018), 52. Isa. 61:2–3; Rev. 21:4. "Jesus Christ overcame the world and 'absorbed' all unfairness. Because of Him, we can have peace in this world and . . . good cheer (John 16:33). If we let Him, Jesus Christ will consecrate the unfairness for our gain (2 Ne. 2:2). He will not just console us and restore what was lost (Job 45:10, 12–13; Jacob 3:1); *He will use the unfairness for our benefit* (Alma 40:5)." Dale G. Renlund, "Infuriating Unfairness," *Liahona*, May 2021, emphasis added, https://www.churchofjesuschrist.org/study/general-conference/2021/04/25renlund?lang=eng. "If we endure our challenges faithfully, they will have no eternal negative consequences for us." Paul V. Johnson, "Free to Choose," *Ensign*, February 2019, https://www.churchofjesuschrist.org/study/ensign/2019/02/free-to-choose?lang=eng.

4. Exod. 2:11–15; Matt. 26:69–75; Mark 14:66–72.
5. "Marriage should not be viewed as a therapeutic step to solve [differences]." Gordon B. Hinckley, "Reverence and Morality," *Ensign*, May 1987, https://www.churchofjesuschrist.org/study/general-conference/1987/04/reverence-and-morality?lang=eng. See also Gospel Topics, "Same Sex Attraction," https://www.churchofjesuschrist.org/study/manual/gospel-topics/same-sex-attraction?lang=eng. Church of Jesus Christ leaders are typically unpaid.
6. Chapter 11 has more insights on why gay men are often promiscuous, generally speaking.
7. According to the CDC, the "percentage of marriages that end in divorce in the US varies between 40% and 50%," and that

number is falling (yet, so is the marriage rate). "The Williams Institute at the UCLA School of Law did publish data which suggested that the same-sex divorce rate was approximately half of the different-sex divorce rate. However, *this was later retracted due to an error* in the calculation of the data." Note that "as same-sex marriages were only recognized on a federal level in the USA in 2013, there is still a lack of data regarding the rate of same-sex divorces." Branka Vuleta, "Divorce Rate in America (35 Stunning Stats for 2022)," Legal Jobs (blog), January 28, 2021, emphasis added, https://legaljobs.io/blog/divorce-rate-in-america/. Some studies show greater satisfaction in gay marriages (than heterosexual) but greater *longevity* in heterosexual marriages; causation will likely be debated long-term. Theresa E. DiDonato, "Are Same-Sex or Heterosexual Relationships More Stable?" Psychology Today (blog), October 11, 2017, https://www.psychologytoday.com/us/blog/meet-catch-and-keep/201710/are-same-sex-or-heterosexual-relationships-more-stable. See also Benjamin R. Karney and Thomas N. Bradbury, "Research on Marital Satisfaction and Stability in the 2010s: Challenging Conventional Wisdom," *Journal of Marriage and Family* 82, no. 1 (January 2020): 100–116, https://doi.org/10.1111/jomf.12635; Lois M. Cochran, "A Religious Upbringing May Reduce Divorce Risk—But Probably Not for the Reason You Think," *Deseret News*, December 18, 2021, https://tinyurl.com/ff6xxtb3.

8. 1 Sam. 18:1–5, 20:16–17, 20:41–42, 23:16–18; 2 Sam. 1:26.
9. John 13:23, 19:25–27. See also Alma 53:2.

10. Joseph B. Wirthlin, "Band of Brothers," *Ensign*, February 2008, https://www.churchofjesuschrist.org/study/ensign/2008/02/band-of-brothers?lang=eng. "I testify that there is a spirit of oneness and of love in the quorum of the twelve, and existing also between them and the presidency of the church, such as you will hardly find among any other men upon earth; a love for one another that almost exceeds the love of a man for his wife." Rudger Clawson, in Conference Report, October 1902, 59, https://archive.org/details/conferencereport1902sa.
11. D&C 130:2.

CHAPTER 8

The Paradox of Sex

"Love ceases to be a demon only when he ceases to be a god."[1]

—M. Denis de Rougemont

NOTE THAT *EROS* IN THESE PASSAGES from C. S. Lewis means classical love and not eroticism:

> Others, with Eros [love] as their fuel and also as their model, can embark on the married life, within which Eros, of himself, will never be enough—will indeed survive only in so far as he is continually chastened and corroborated by higher principles.
>
> But Eros honoured without reservation and obeyed unconditionally, becomes a demon. And this is just how he claims to be honoured and obeyed. Divinely indifferent to our selfishness, he is also demoniacally rebellious to every claim of God or Man that would oppose him. Hence, as the poet says: "People in love cannot be moved by kindness, And opposition makes them feel like martyrs."[2]

EUPHORIA

I'm finally going to address the questions that began chapter 5, specifically the question of same-sex relationships in the Church of Jesus Christ and the misconception that same-sex attraction presents a binary choice: either to leave your faith and embrace a fully sexualized gay lifestyle or to stay in the church, suppress your feelings, and remain alone. To avoid missing empowering insights, I encourage you to read this chapter in one sitting. Pardon that much of this comes from the male point of view, as it is the only one I have. As you read, you might prayerfully ask God to help you discern truth from any error.

I believe that sex (or mutual activities that tend to result in sexual climax) opens not only the heart but also one's very spirit. When sex occurs as God intended it, He is involved, and it can be a transcendent, bonding thing. I acknowledge that male-female sex may not currently be that—even for some heterosexual people, and even in covenant marriages.

Sex outside the Lord's scant guidelines *also* opens the spirit . . . to other influences. I want to be clear: I am convinced that sex without God's blessing is sex where negative influences have access to your opened, vulnerable spirit. This can be so in cisgender heterosexual relations—even in heterosexual married sex! I *don't* believe sex is only for procreation, but some sex is not mutually agreed on, appropriate, or cherished by both participants, and it's detrimental to the intimacy of the relationship.[3]

Can "inappropriate" sex feel good? Absolutely, and intensely so. Still, what some call "love" is temporary euphoria resulting from sex. Euphoria is a transitory feeling within the self; it is not connection with another. While it might accompany love, euphoria is *not* love.[4] There is danger of real tragedy in confusing euphoria for love—also in exalting even true love above anything else. C. S. Lewis wrote:

> Of all loves [Eros] is, at his height, most god-like; therefore most prone to demand our worship. Of himself he always tends to turn "being in love" into a sort of religion. . . .
>
> "Love made us do it," notice the tone. A man saying "I did it because I was frightened," or "I did it because I was angry," speaks quite differently. . . . But lovers are seldom doing quite that. Notice how tremulously, almost how devoutly, they say the word *love*, not so much pleading in an "extenuating circumstance" as appealing to an authority. The confession can be almost a boast. There can be a shade of defiance in it. They "feel like martyrs." In extreme cases what their words really express is a demure yet unshakable allegiance to the god of love. They are now under a new law. . . . The "spirit" of Eros supersedes all laws, and they must not [offend] it. . . .
>
> It seems to sanction all sorts of actions they would not otherwise have dared. I do not mean solely, or chiefly, acts that violate chastity. They are just as likely to be acts of injustice or uncharity against the outer

> world. They will seem like proofs of piety and zeal towards Eros. The pair can say to one another in an almost sacrificial spirit, "It is for love's sake that I have neglected my parents—left my children—cheated my partner—failed my friend at his greatest need." These reasons in love's law have passed for good. The [devotees] may even come to feel a particular merit in such sacrifices; what costlier offering can be laid on love's altar than one's own conscience?[5]

Apart from the harm that comes from exalting true love above all other considerations, confusing transitory euphoria for love is almost a guarantee that a person will fall *out* of "love" due to the fleeting nature of the emotion.

I say this having repeatedly experienced emptiness and pain by opening my soul to influences God never wanted for me. Here, I am *not* speaking of cultural guilt from my upbringing; before I ever felt any guilt or shame from my religion over my sexual activity, I had already experienced the hollowness that follows transitory sexual euphoria. I was not taught that premarital *or* gay sex could be damaging before I began acting sexually; I didn't even know what sex was at the time, but I experienced the natural letdown and ache all the same. Nobody wants their loved ones to suffer these negative influences and non-bonding outcomes; if we encourage sexual activities that *aren't* mutual, affirming, opposite-sex spousal acts, our words are misleading, perhaps harmful.[6]

Something to contemplate: The *lasting* benefit in the "act of creation" (the gift of intimacy) can't occur when the Creator and His purposes are ignored, shunned, or slighted. I'm not simplistically stating that all heterosexual sex is good and gay sex is bad; I'm saying God has declared a way in which sex can be an instrument of divine bonding, and *any* other use of sex seems to lead to disappointment, if not harm—heterosexual or gay or other.

MORE IS NOT MORE

I've known *a lot* of gay men!

I've experienced firsthand euphoric excitement with men. The biggest puzzle for me has been that sex between men doesn't seem to bond a pair as it can unite some opposite-sex couples (though not *all* heterosexual couples). I don't pretend to know why; my working theory is that men and women can bond sexually long-term because they are sufficiently dissimilar.

I'm not saying that lasting connection doesn't exist between people of the same sex, only that when it happens, it seems to happen a *different way* than with heterosexual couples.[7]

While exhilarating (sometimes electric!), sexual stimulation between men seems to lead to emotional distancing—though, at first, it feels like connection, and the euphoria can last for days. I think men often do establish true emotional connection with each other; then, based on the more-is-more fallacy, they get sexual and, evidently, obliterate the linkage. I have experienced this again and again. Some men openly acknowledge that they use sex to *avoid* intimacy.[8]

Many gay men remain bewildered by the lack of a true union between themselves and their significant others. A lot of couples remain silent, thinking they are the anomaly among many happy gay pairs, but they are like other sexual gay partners: disconnected. In my observation, even gay married couples in the first weeks of sexual euphoria (much mistaken for love) seem to crash into the reality of separateness, unless (ironically) they stop being sexual and nourish the unique bonding expressions of God-given same-sex connection.

My friend Mica from California never acted sexually with men in his first thirty-five years of life because he grew up in a tight group of buddies that camped, played, and hung out together. It was much like the comradery that nourished my same-sex emotional needs while I was a missionary for two years. These close male connections met his true needs until they married off and became busy with families. After moving to Utah—even farther from that nourishment—Mica had some euphoric gay trysts, then married a man. Only *weeks* into his marriage, he acknowledged that the flame between him and his husband was already gone.

Of course, there are many unhappy heterosexual couples and many who have divorced: Wedded bliss is elusive for both heterosexuals and gays. Yet, the loss of union that can occur with heterosexual married couples seems universal (by my observations) between people whose sexual acts by nature open the spirit to negative influences—straight, gay, or otherwise—in what one might otherwise expect to be a very intimate link. Though the distance need not be irreparable.

There is one caveat: Dependence or overreliance on euphoria can give the *illusion* of connectedness, making a person feel they have a deep union with another—and making them quite reluctant to give up a sexual partner. (It can be excruciatingly difficult, at least, in the first days of euphoria.) Have you ever done something to a partner that you knew they wouldn't like, but you felt it was too exciting to resist? Expressions preceded by "Just let me . . ." are often a red flag that your gratification—not love—is your motivation. Your "bond" may actually be dependence on the high of orgasm. Self-focused gratification (not surrendered to God) can increase personal appetites in a compounding way that never satisfies. Wanting more always leads to wanting more. Many guys who believed they had a good bond with a partner were surprised to find themselves acting sexually with another person (their true same-sex needs weren't being met—by the partner or in the tryst).

Some couples, gay and heterosexual, resort to novel sexual experiences in an attempt to regain their bond. In the past, I have been invited into "marital activities" by gay couples. They didn't appear to be into each other much and seemed to hope to preserve the union by adding me to mix. Good as it is, sexual euphoria can't fulfill real needs, and it doesn't last, which is why so many guys with partners seek outside guys; they think they've lost love when it is actually euphoria that has faded. All the while, the soul continues to crave true same-sex connection.

But giving up a partner isn't always necessary (unless that person is unwilling to look at nonsexual options). My friend Jaime and his male partner have been together for more than sixteen years—and they're deeply united in love. They haven't been sexual with each other for many years, and neither seems interested in pairing with anyone else. I'm convinced that their relationship has lasted not in spite of ending the sex, but *because* of it: They've grown into a deeper connection than what sex brought them, and their bond is no longer threatened by the post-euphoria distancing of homosexual sex.

If you know of a gay couple wherein both partners still genuinely cherish each other—prefer each other's company over other options after twenty or more years—I would wager they are no longer being sexual, though they more than likely reinforce their union with affection.

Pardon the metaphor, but same-sex touch is like rubbing alcohol: so soothing on the skin, not so great taken internally! True lasting connection is heavenly. When we try to deepen it with orgasms, there's euphoria for a bit, then an isolating sickness of the soul, as from ingesting something intended to soothe topically. As with street drugs, people seek more of what makes them sick—euphoria or specious connection—even from strangers;

you'll likely want this, as I did, if your "hits" have included sexual stimulation. The relationships around you and me seem to bear this out.

Our gay friends' blissful posts on social media only show the electric euphoria, never the letdowns and putting themselves on the market again and again, chasing fulfilment of legitimate needs in a wasteland of sex—apparently extinguishing budding connections via sexual relating. Even for people who put off sex until they are in love, it appears that same-sex sexual behavior interferes with lasting bonding.

I'm not persuaded that gay sexual partnerships fail because of societal disapproval. I grew up in the San Francisco Bay Area; not only was "free love" preached there all my years, but so was gay life. Some Bible Belt communities may have condemned gayness regularly, but that hasn't been the norm in my California turf for some time. Even in that tolerant environment, I observed that even exclusive gay partnerships that didn't discover nonsexual bonding tended to fizzle out (as did most "open" ones).

Many gay couples, some together for decades, have made accommodations driven by the quest for ongoing euphoria by opening up their marriages or overlooking cheating. By contrast, I personally know multiple happy gay couples that are no longer sexual, yet they have been bonded for a decade or more.

I'm not declaring that one hundred percent of sexual gay partnerships fail as far as monogamy or union (though it wouldn't surprise me), but I ask—rhetorically—what have you observed? Is the long-term happy couple you know faithful and sexual, or might they now be enjoying something better than gay sex? How united are those in open marriages? My point isn't to prove or disprove the existence of a long-term faithful and sexual gay couple. The important question for a great many of us is this: Even if a gay couple exists that is happily monogamous and sexual for twenty or more years, given the scarcity of examples, might my coming suggestions for lasting same-sex fulfillment be well founded and worth your time?

PAIRING PATHS

I know firsthand the lack of fulfillment many of us have experienced while trying to establish same-sex bonds sexually, so I cannot sincerely congratulate anyone entering such a partnership. I will wish couples every happiness, but internally, I don't celebrate something I've observed to distance people from each other.

Some people have told me, "You just haven't had sex with the right man," or "You weren't in love." I'm not saying men can't love other men, because I certainly do, nor am I saying there is no pleasure or euphoria in "unchaste" sex, only that there seems to be something in homosexual sex that is counter to the true connection we're seeking. More importantly, there's something superior in nonsexual same-sex welds that promotes and *reinforces* lasting relations. It took me years to put my finger on the difference, but it all comes back to shedding the gradual (or immediate) post-euphoric emptiness and isolation I've described above and choosing a bond that can be limitless in depth and duration. I'm discussing outcomes that are not necessarily God-imposed: equal and opposite reactions we can only temporarily ignore. Some are obvious; some take time to appreciate.

Today, I enjoy profound, lasting male connection. In coming chapters, I'll detail how to create enduring union with people of one's own sex.

While I have poignant personal feelings on sexual gay unions, I've rarely dissuaded persons who are determined to act—though I will share my experience if asked (sometimes when I am not asked). For some of us, there is no other way to comprehend or be persuaded about something than to experience it (hopefully not on perpetual replay). God has always allowed us to evaluate for ourselves; our agency is sacred. I also know that no damage need be permanent (see chapter 5), though we might miss out on some blessings as we stubbornly struggle to learn from our own experiences.

Can same-sex links be repaired? Yes. People of the same sex, regardless of sexual orientation, are designed to love each other powerfully and in distinct ways from opposite-sex pairings. Same-sex connection eroded by sex can be repaired by embracing the unique same-sex bonding that meets legitimate needs, the (often overlooked) expressions that facilitate the deepest, most resilient same-sex connection.

SACRED COW

Though I'm not an authority on bonding in heterosexual marriages, I've observed some similarities and differences with same-sex couples. When I say that some heterosexual sexual couples find lasting connection and people of the same sex find it in nonsexual ways, my naive impression is that those heterosexual pairs seem to stumble into union by chance. (I really don't know how it happens—it seems random to me. Even when both partners work hard at the marriage, only some of them bond.) I've happily observed that people of the same sex—regardless of orientation—appear to be *wired* with the potential for deep union with each other (even if they also enjoy a spousal relationship with someone of the opposite sex). This seems to be by design for individual and general joy.

In many cultures, sex isn't the highest expression of love. Many heterosexual couples will affirm that sex does not necessarily equate to intimacy and that unity—not sex—is the top benefit to their relationship.[9]

Overall, I challenge society's sacred cow of sex. I've had many sexual experiences, and I've lived decades without sex. I disagree that nothing is better than sex, that one cannot survive without sex, and I disagree that the ultimate expression of love is sex. Please scrutinize John 15:12–13.

IS SEX A NEED?

Imagine you're indefinitely stuck halfway down a hole, unable to reach anything below your waist (yet you can urinate and defecate). Within reach is all the food and water you'll ever need. Will you perish from deprivation of any sort? Nope. While you might experience great yearning—even torment yourself in the first couple years that you're going crazy or dying from lack of sex—you'd soon learn it isn't so. This scenario is unappealing (thank heaven most of us can move about!), but it illustrates that your greatest deprivation would be psychological—if you were deprived of human social relating.

My point is that our social needs are critical. Sex is wonderful (and a want). Emotional connections are a need, and only when bonding needs are met can sex be understood and valued for its merits.

Loving someone doesn't always mean it's best to be sexual with that person (it may not be good for you or for the other person). Married heterosexual people still need to control physical appetites, free-love advocates can't have sex whenever they want, and even the uber-wealthy discover that they can't have all they want whenever they want it. Some of the most difficult trials for heterosexual people through history also involve not being with the person they most loved—and many of the most satisfying relationships were never sexual.[10]

Some people sabotage God-given connectedness by presuming that any kind of love expression, or escalation of expression, increases or deepens their connection. There are love expressions that build bonds between mother and daughter, friends, siblings, father and son, husband and wife, and so on, expressions that—in one scenario—build connection, yet the same expressions might *diminish* bonding in other situations. Disciplining our desires and love expressions appropriately allows us to cultivate our various relationships.[11]

Some people have expressed pity that I currently don't experience sexual satisfaction with someone. Some have intimated to me that perhaps I'm in denial about my desires and need to own them; this suggestion implies that I haven't tried their way of living and presumes that I haven't explored my feelings. These opinions can be surprising for me to hear; after nearly five decades of contemplating my attractions and varied relations, I've encountered a path that fulfills me more than gay sexual relationships ever did—this seems like considerable rumination. As good as orgasm can be, I pity those who've never experienced deep, abiding union because their fixation on sexual euphoria has prevented them from progressing to deeper human connection.

Are LGBTQIA people and those who never desire a heterosexual union consigned to misery by God or the Church of Jesus Christ?[12] Are gays condemned to never have a "soulmate"?[13] If the person closest to you in life and in eternity is the same sex as you, will that bar you from eternal joy? Not at all!

My own experience tells me that sexuality (and, I suspect, gender identity) can be fluid. What may repel you today may attract you in some future year or in eternity—though a heterosexual union is *not* required to live eternally with God and loved ones.

People in mystifying situations might question God's love for them. Don't doubt—He has stated and demonstrated His love for us again and again.[14] Romantic "love" isn't optimal relating for couples of any orientation—even sexual expression can't hold a candle to lasting, immutable union. Isn't much of the pain we experience in our lives the result of comparison and unrealistic expectations? Life is too short to waste on needless anguish. If you don't want marriage with the opposite sex, you have other wondrous relationship options here and now. We also have an eternity of relating ahead![15]

Why might a loving parent ask someone to delay something? In the big picture, there are numerous valid reasons, but it is never to deprive us; it is always to endow us with more than what we expect or want. I've learned that fulfilling relationships are always God's desire for us—and possible in *this* life—even if we don't marry here.[16]

I appeal to the expert on you: *you*. Look back over your life and honestly assess your emotions and relationships. Taking all feelings into account (not just sexual euphoria), over the long run, how bonded have you remained to persons of your sex with whom you continue to be sexual? Perhaps take some weeks or months to come to a conclusion and an opinion for yourself on the odds for long-term same-sex bonding (sexual versus nonsexual). Even if you and the most important person in your life were sexual in the past, perhaps you're now enjoying the lasting nonsexual ties I speak of.

I've learned that resilient, fulfilling relationships are not just for a few heterosexual couples. Just about anyone can find union. My deepest, most rewarding relationships resulted from the loss of relations and unmet expectations that I previously held as important. Your best relationships may not be the one(s) you're currently in or pursuing or think you're missing out on (or they may not come about in the way you're trying to build them). I suspect that many more women (straight, lesbian, and queer) and heterosexual men have experienced the same-sex bonding joys I'm discussing than have gay men (a big reason I wrote this book is because *I* was distracted from these insights for too long). There are more factors for your consideration ahead; ultimately, you must be the judge.

POINTS TO PONDER

- Everyone has multiple human relation options. Your most rewarding relationships may not be the ones you think you're missing. Seeing abundant options might require modification to current notions. It's possible that the person you have the deepest connection to—now and in eternity—is the same sex as you.
- Emotional connection is a need. Sex is not love and doesn't satisfy true needs. Confusing euphoria for

love often leads to falling out of "love" due to the fleeting nature of the emotion. How else have you found emotional connections in your relationships?

- Inappropriate or selfish sex—heterosexual or otherwise—disconnects us from the joy of union (and can be torture to escape; wanting more always leads to wanting more). In particular, sexual stimulation between people of the same sex appears to result in emotional distancing—even for those who wait until they're in love. How might this effort to create a bond have the opposite effect?
- Many have experienced the profound connection that can endure between people of the same sex who *avoid* being sexual with each other. Same-sex bonds can be repaired. There are happy gay couples who are not sexual yet are truly united for decades. What other welds might be at work in these relationships?

NOTES

1. "Love ceases to be a demon only when it ceases to be a god." M. Denis de Rougemont, RightWords.eu, YourCHOICE, accessed August 19, 2022, https://rightwords.eu/quotes/love-ceases-to-be-a-demon-only-when-it-ceases-to-be-a-god--31669.
2. Lewis, *The Four Loves*, 6.
3. God has given scriptural guidelines on successful relating to save us time and heartache on painful paths. Read these verses in the context of one another. (I acknowledge

that some Bible verses historically thought to be against homosexuality in fact speak against pedophilia; yet, there are many scriptures that warn—for our own fulfillment—against sexual acts between adults of the same sex.) See Gen. 1:22, 1:27–28, 2:24, 19, 37–38, 39:1–18; Exod. 20:14; Lev. 18:20–22, 20:10–13; Num. 25:1; Deut. 5:18; 1 Kings 14:24; 2 Kings 23:7; Ps. 51:10, 119:9; Prov. 31:10; Matt. 5:27–28, 15:19, 19:4–9; Mark 10:2–12; Acts 15:19–20; Rom. 1:18–32, 2:22, 13:13; 1 Cor. 7:2–9, 5:9–11, 6:9–11, 6:18-20, 10:8; Eph. 5:3, 28–31; 1 Thess. 4:3; 1 Tim. 1:8–11; 2 Tim. 2:22; Titus 2:4–12; 1 Pet. 2:11; Jude 7; Rev. 2:14, 9:21, 14:1–5; Jacob 2:28; Alma 13:28, Alma 39; D&C 121:45.

4. Euphoria is a sense of pleasure—even temporary joy—like a drug high. Because it is chemically induced, it cannot last. I've lost count of the sexually partnered gay men I've met who are no longer experiencing the euphoria they called "love." See also *Merriam-Webster.com Dictionary*, s.v. "euphoria," accessed August 8, 2022, https://www.merriam-webster.com/dictionary/euphoria.
5. "And all the time the grim joke is that this Eros whose voice seems to speak from the eternal realm is not himself necessarily even permanent. He is notoriously the most mortal of our loves. . . . Our natural loves [are] rivals to the love of God. . . . When God arrives (and only then) the half-gods can [take their proper places]. Left to themselves they either vanish or become demons. Only in His name can they with beauty and security 'wield their little tridents.' The rebellious slogan 'All for love' is really love's death warrant." Lewis, *The Four Loves*, 92, 110–15, 118–19.
6. Please see Epilogue.

7. Could it be possible that oxytocin, the feel-good/bonding hormone released in cuddling and sex, doesn't seem to affect same-sex couples in the same ways it affects heterosexual couples? My experience is that feeling good happens for both, but bonding, not so much with same-sex sex. I believe that something other than chemical reaction is going on. See also Stephanie Watson, "Oxytocin: The Love Hormone," Harvard Health Publishing, July 20, 2021, https://www.health.harvard.edu/mind-and-mood/oxytocin-the-love-hormone.
8. One definition of *intimacy* is "belonging to or characterizing one's deepest nature." *Merriam-Webster.com Dictionary*, s.v. "intimacy," accessed August 8, 2022, https://www.merriam-webster.com/dictionary/intimate.
9. Family life professor Stephen F. Duncan cites the National Health and Social Life Survey: "About 20 percent of [heterosexual] couples at any age have a nonsexual marriage." M. Sue Bergin, "Don't Let Your Marriage Go Cold," *BYU Magazine*, March 2020, https://magazine.byu.edu/article/dont-let-your-marriage-go-cold/. And it's not necessarily a bad thing: See Jennifer Harbutt, "'I Don't Think We'll Ever Have Sex Again': Our Happy, Cuddly, Celibate Marriage," *The Guardian*, April 15, 2017, https://www.theguardian.com/lifeandstyle/2017/apr/15/celibate-marriage-sex-sexless-relationship. See also Edward O. Laumann et al., "National Health and Social Life Survey, 1992: [United States]," Inter-university Consortium for Political and Social Research (April 17, 2008), https://doi.org/10.3886/ICPSR06647.v2.
10. Ask several people about the person they were or are closest

to and (if they're comfortable saying) whether it was a sexual relationship. This can be an illuminating exercise.

11. Jails and hospitals have a number of people in them who at some point presumed that *any* expression of love in any scenario is only a positive thing. Many people are hooked on the *idea* of sex with a particular person. Real life, films, and fiction are filled with examples of relationship tragedy—not because society created the consequences but because mistrust, neglect, depression, and jealousy are natural consequences of infidelity. See David A. Bednar, "Watchful unto Prayer Continually," *Ensign*, November 2019, https://www.churchofjesuschrist.org/study/general-conference/2019/10/22bednar?lang=eng.
12. Why might some people suppose they might be tested in any area except when it comes to love—or if their test has to do with relationships, they are being singled out? It's easy to feel isolated in a struggle with unwanted or unsatisfied desire, to look inward without recognizing that many people have similar or parallel frustrations. Some people mistakenly believe those with physical or mental limitations, the widowed, or the aged may not have a sex drive. It's also untrue that every married person is content, with all their sexual and intimate needs met. I'm not saying same-sex attraction is no worse or somehow better than another situation, only that each of us has unique circumstances that might cause us difficulty, cause us to question God's concern for our needs and desires. Without worrying whether our varied difficulties are more or less or equally painful, our discipleship to Christ leads us to be compassionate to each other's pain. "Beloved, think it not strange concerning

the fiery trial which is to try you, as though some [isolated] thing happened unto you: But rejoice." 1 Pet. 4:12–13.

13. "I'm not sure *anyone* lives in that perfect, ideal family. . . . My own experiences have sometimes brought me bright pain and concentrated loneliness. It's easy to blame that pain on the category of my life circumstances, but I've come to see that everyone is dealing with pain. . . . It's the state of mortality. The best we can do is try to help bear each other's pain." Sharon Eubank, "A Letter to a Single Sister," *Ensign*, March 2020, 40–41.
14. Jer. 31:3; John 3:16–17; Rom. 8:31–39.
15. Mark 16:16. If you want children in eternity, and you continue to look to Christ, you will have them—and you'll be pleased with the means by which they come. See Matt. 19:29; Mark 10:30. "In the Lord's own way and time, no blessing will be withheld from His faithful Saints. The Lord will judge and reward each individual according to heartfelt desire as well as deed." Russell M. Nelson, "Celestial Marriage," *Ensign*, October 2008, 94. Please see endnote 5 in chapter 6.
16. Nelson, 94. Some people's decisions are harder than others; still, I think everyone will, in the end, acknowledge that their circumstances were suited to them and facilitated the best opportunities for growth and self-discovery (unfolding happiness). Being true to one's heart should never mean abandoning facts. Relationships (simply) based on emotion tend to be disjointed, dysfunctional, and fragile, as opposed to those based on character and commitment, where devotion is to the *union*, not necessarily to the partner (more disciplined, yet with a better success rate; unwavering commitment to the *partner* may not be possible on all days).

CHAPTER 9
Beyond Grief—What If I Don't Have Support?

The appendixes of this book have excellent resources for LGBTQIA persons and those that love them. For perspective, I'm including some personal events that taught me that the loss of some things we hold dear can open us to receiving far better things.

As YEARS PASSED AFTER MY MISSION, my stomach distress worsened, becoming constant and painful; it seemed whatever I ate made things worse. Carbohydrates brought agony.

When my oldest brother was diagnosed, at eighteen years old, with diabetes, I remember thinking, "I could never go without sugar!" Today, my diet is more restricted than his. I live on meat, eggs, and vegetables. I struggle to keep weight on, my gut remains tender, and I have to ration my energy. People express envy for my svelte body, but I tell them they wouldn't want to pay what I pay for it!

Despite all kinds of scans, tests, cleanses, antibiotics, antiparasitics, and visits to Stanford Medical Center and countless doctors, no one has identified or remedied the problem. If I eat carbs (this is the trigger, *not* stress, *not* guilt), the pain can increase to torture. I've lost track of the money spent on doctors and medicine, but I know which foods bring torment, and I'm satisfied the cause is purely physiological and not psychological.

Unsure I could continue an independent life for long, I returned to Utah to be closer to family (most live here now). It was a blessing. Not long after my arrival, my appendix burst, and I had family around me after emergency surgery.

I built myself a vibrant life in Utah. I had several books published, got engaged to a woman (though we later broke it off), got a master's degree, and began teaching college media courses. At the same time, I suffered increasing anxiety because I no longer had confidence in my ability to control my body. My professional and social lives were impacted by the fear of what might come out of my body at inopportune moments. I was dating, but each date was first stressful, then, eventually, a major effort (and sometimes humiliating). Soon, I would return from short dates completely exhausted.

I told the Lord I no longer had the energy to look for the right woman. I also had to alter my work to something I could do at home. Since I had been freelancing and had some books out, publishing became my focus. I was happy to find success, but it was lonely. My family and a couple of married friends became my only social contacts; they're wonderful and I love them, but that level of human contact wasn't enough.

It appears Satan wanted me to isolate. Isolation is the worst thing for an addict, but it's pretty bad for just about anyone; neediness can ambush you in random casual human interactions.[1]

It can be difficult to be sick and appear healthy. People in hospital beds don't get the same judgments as those of us who only appear well; I may be on my feet and participating, but I can't do everything a healthy person can. Sometimes I feel judged or misunderstood. All the same, despite my ignorance of a remedy, Heavenly Father has kept me functioning for years. No matter the discomfort, so far, I've had the energy to do the essential things. Still, my closest encounter with Jesus Christ happened in my deepest physical suffering—I will never regret that experience.

IT'S "NOT GOOD" TO BE ALONE

The move to Utah also brought me closer to certain judgments and the opportunity to come to terms with them. A few years ago, I learned that the brother just older than me has disapproved of me for some time. Though he considers himself an ally of LGBTQIA people, he doesn't feel his bi younger brother can offer him any insights on the topic.

It was particularly devastating to feel misunderstood by someone who has heard firsthand the messy details of my activities with men—yet who, apparently, doesn't know me. For years, I've sought peace with God and those around me, and I've learned much. Despite my openness about my past and my experiences, this brother dismisses, judges, and denounces me (mostly since cleaning up my act twenty-five years ago). Being misjudged is painful; being wrongly condemned by someone who should know me well and has professed love is worse.[2]

I no longer feel affirmed at some family gatherings. Even when I'm present in body, I'm guarded, and it can be lonely. While dejected, my attitude is that I must forgive. I anticipate enjoying all of my family when they love again. Some growth may only come in the next life.

I'm comforted knowing that God meant all of this for my good. My poor health and faltering family support did increase my isolation. Still, all these difficulties combined gave me time to rest and evaluate my relationships. Without these "setbacks," I would never have embarked on the discovery I'm writing about. I never dreamed relationships could be so rewarding until I'd lost poor ones that I'd clung to.

Perhaps you feel, as I did, that you could never live without carbs (or whatever you most delight in). I'm here to say that some of our most poignant losses often lead to gains far beyond what we so treasured before. Satan loves for us to feel hopeless about our situations, almost as much as he loves for us to isolate, but God can turn our most painful difficulties into blessings.

In 2018, I felt led by God to expand my social circle in a new way. For me, tragedy brought me to the best chapter of my life.

POINTS TO PONDER

- Transitory euphoria cannot fulfill true needs (the self is never satisfied). What have you found that meets your real needs?
- Isolation is bad for just about anyone and worse for those of us trying to change behavior or overcome addiction. What tools and resources can you turn to when you feel isolated?
- Making sincere efforts to progress doesn't necessarily shield you from judgment and misunderstandings, even from those you want most to understand you. How can your relationship with God and others help you with this kind of discouragement?

NOTES

1. Gen. 2:18.
2. "Many people today . . . are either unable to see things as they truly are or are unsatisfied with the truth. Moreover, there are forces at play today designed to deliberately lead us away from absolute truth. These deceptions and lies . . . often have dire, not minor, consequences." Gary E. Stevenson, "Deceive Me Not," *Ensign*, October 2019, https://www.churchofjesuschrist.org/study/general-conference/2019/10/45stevenson?lang=eng.

CHAPTER 10

The Best News—How to Create Deep Same-Sex Connection

"We crave to be touched, looked at, admired, smiled at—to laugh with and feel safe."[1]

—Counselor Marshal Burtcher

I HAVE A STARTLING SECRET TO SHARE with you: You don't have to battle your libido, you don't have to repress it, and you don't have to surrender to your sex drive as the ruler of your life—it's *not* your enemy. Your libido can work for you as a helpful, though rudimentary, gauge that lets you know when you're neglecting human relating needs. Here's a roundabout explanation:

I postulate that sex is the thief of lasting same-sex connection. Lots of people (including my past self) get sexual primarily because they know of no other way to connect with those of their own sex. It is amazing how many people have gone through life—as I did for years—believing there are only two paths to experiencing same-sex attraction: try to enjoy sex with someone of my sex or give up same-sex emotional needs entirely. For many years, I sought fulfillment in same-sex sexual relating, and while I experienced physical gratification, I never found the deep connection I sought. Rejecting that approach, I tried being a recluse. I also tried to marry the opposite sex, a solution which carries the possibility of giving up same-sex needs. All of these approaches left me hollow and discouraged, but I came to believe there had to be other options out there.

I was looking for something fulfilling that creates deep bonds, that acknowledges the nuances of my same-sex needs and lets me be informed by my libido rather than denying it or giving in to its immediate clamoring. There is an option that fills me better than any of those first either/or choices. It is deep, lasting union—and can be found in more ways than I describe here. I encourage you to find connection that meets your God-given needs.[2]

MEETING GOD-GIVEN SAME-SEX EMOTIONAL NEEDS

After ten years of isolation, God pushed me back into society. (I hadn't been a total hermit, but contacts with just a few family members and friends were insufficient.) While I'm sure I'd had at least a passing awareness of it before, I was now quite aware of how much I had lacked for human touch. I had begun to feel resentment when greeting people: I would think, "That's a polite handshake, but an embrace would be better." My body and brain were signaling to me that I had an unmet need for physical connection and that it wasn't necessarily a sexual one.

I realized I had to accept people where they were with what they were willing to give; I also intuited that somewhere out there were people whose desire for emotional connection and affection was as great as mine, regardless of their sexual orientation. I started searching for platonic and asexual social sites. They were not easy to find. Eventually, I found a couple of them, but their few members were scattered around the globe.[3]

While I feared I might revert to compulsive sexual activity, I felt that God was leading me in this new direction. Though many sites declared themselves "nonsexual," each person I met still had to be vetted as to their true motivations. I eventually found a couple of local people who agreed to respect my boundaries.

Not everyone believed that all I wanted was to talk and embrace, and nothing sexual. But articulating my boundaries and sticking to them went a long way in making me credible and having people honor my objectives.

My first acquaintance in my nonsexual connection experiment had come from out of town and was staying in a hotel. I made him wait twenty-four hours after agreeing to meet! I wasn't sure that he, like me, only wanted emotional connection and affection. I wasn't sure how I'd do, either; I was concerned that I'd revert to old habits and violate the boundaries each of us had set. It had been years since I'd been sexual, and I didn't want to return to that insatiable lifestyle. When I met Tony at his hotel room, I asked to prop the door to the room wide open, and we remained clothed.

What happened next had never happened to me in all my previous (sexual) experiences—but it's a regular and constant part of my life now. No sooner did I realize that Tony wasn't after sex (I already knew I wasn't) than we opened up and bonded *profoundly*. The conversation was natural, and the connection and physical affection were so pleasant, it all seemed almost otherworldly.

I had felt deep yearning and passion for guys in my past. I believe I had initiated bonding with some men, but it always seemed to evaporate. Now, I know that dissipation happened after we got sexual—which was typically the pattern back then. This time, my "neediness" wasn't the priority, and it never became so. What I experienced was a near-total feeling of love and concern for Tony and a desire that he feel completely loved and accepted. I still feel that for him; we've remained very close to this day. Our first meeting was in 2018, and though Tony's from the Midwest, he visits Utah regularly.

Reflecting later, I searched my memory more deeply and remembered I *had* experienced such bonding, years before. When I was a young man, I had a church buddy who was very nurturing and affectionate but with whom

I was never sexual. He and I had shared this same kind of bond, though I hadn't appreciated it for what it was at the time.

NEVER IN A MILLION YEARS

Same-sex connection isn't about finding a soul mate—though I'm not saying that couldn't happen—nor is it about playing around or using a person. It's about making my relationships as lasting and rewarding as possible. Male love isn't a zero-sum thing (more on this in the next chapter).

Embracing a person nonsexually offers emotional and spiritual nourishment and can result in feelings of contentment and peace. Done right, holding and being held leaves a person feeling fulfilled—rather than hungry for sex. As long as the embrace is not sexualized, it can establish lasting emotional connectedness and deep intimacy without clinginess or dependence; compare this to a burst of sexual euphoria followed by a gradual or immediate loss of connection.[4]

Because the connection is with my gender, it is unique compared to other pairings or groupings. It's not sexual; its nature is deeper than friendship, beyond platonic, yet it's not spousal or other-halved. Significantly, it's not necessarily exclusive (though one-on-one *at a time* is best). It's the affirming exchanges that please independent of sexual relating. It establishes a genuine bond. If you reevaluate your relationships and previous expectations in light of the fulfilling nature of these unique connections, you may note that possessiveness and jealousy fade from the picture (see chapter 11).

In our culture, it's easy to miss beneficial experiences that satisfy our emotional appetites. So many of us—especially men!—are starving. More than one man has said to me that he'd never before experienced the depth of love felt while receiving safe affection from someone who understood his needs and wasn't trying to be sexual. Many men experience the exact epiphany that I did in holding—declaring to me, "*This* is what I've always wanted, but I never realized it until now!" (I suspect that many of us as youth were indeed aware of this true desire early on, but it was quickly eclipsed by the euphoria and distraction of sex.)

Heterosexual people also need same-sex connection, regardless of whether it involves physical affection. At a Sexaholics Anonymous (twelve-step) meeting, I met a man who struggled with pornography and lust for women. L.J. seemed tough, almost stern; I approached him with the hope of expanding my social circle (he, obviously, knew of my past compulsions with men). Not long after becoming friends, I explained to him my quest for nonsexual contact. L.J. shook his head and essentially said, "Never in a million years will that happen between you and me."

A couple months later, L.J. and I were sitting in his garage (I'd helped him move something there), and he put his arm around me. I put mine around him—then he wept.

The surprise of contact with this resolutely heterosexual man was eclipsed by my utter astonishment at his reaction (though I just sat with him, hoping not to show surprise). I learned that day that just about anyone can experience deep need for affection from those of their sex. In fact, week after week, L.J. would invite me over, and we would sit and talk with arms around each other (sometimes with his wife chatting with us). I've since held other heterosexual men. All humans need connection and touch.

BOUNDARIES: TRUE CONNECTION'S PARADOX

Before any holding happens, all boundaries and desired outcomes should be articulated clearly by both people (recall that emotional need can manifest as sexual desire). Forgive my bluntness, but one of the best ways people understand that I am serious about not wanting to be sexual is to stay clothed. Touching skin can be healthful, but not wearing any clothing can easily be misinterpreted; one or both partners are susceptible to being sidetracked sexually. Even if one feels completely confident that they won't get sexual, that doesn't address the *other* person's feelings of vulnerability—not to mention what proximity and nakedness combined might trigger in either person's mind.[5]

It's inappropriate and defeats the purpose of holding to be in a situation where even one person is uncomfortable. Naked holding can be the result of social pressure, which is totally inappropriate and incongruent with the objectives of holding and certainly with those of sex: Consent, not coercion, is at the root of all healthful and respectful interactions.[6] If you are sincere about nonsexual holding, don't propose or agree to combine it with nudity. Comfortable pants or shorts and a T-shirt can provide a helpful boundary.

Having more than one holding partner can help avoid too much reliance on any one person. Still, keep it to one partner at a time; my experience is that true connection is quite unlikely with more than two people present.

Both parties should articulate their needs and desires and decide together how holding might look for them (sitting side by side or in other positions). Make it understood that neither person will grab or rub against the groin or other sensitive areas of the other person or attempt to sexually arouse themselves or the other person.

Holding in silence for a time is fine, but if there is never conversation, a person might begin to fixate on bodies. Discover each other's stories, what each is learning or experiencing; laugh together. The objective here is emotional connection: While touch can be a wonderful expression of affection, it shouldn't become the object.[7]

Even while holding, flexibility and rigidity have their place. Just because connecting was done one way doesn't mean it has to continue that way. You may discover that some things don't work or would be better than what has been articulated; speak your mind. Feel free to remind a person of your boundaries; you may need to physically move—or move part of their body—to maintain boundaries. Open communication is vital. Never assume that any individual is impervious to lust. Always speak up if something is not comfortable for you, and never rely on another person to maintain your boundaries; that is always your responsibility.[8] A caveat: While it is essential for you to keep your own boundaries, this should never have to be a battle. Your cuddle partner must understand and support your limits. If your holding companion has a problem with changes or with respecting boundaries, you may need to find someone else.[9]

Physical arousal is not uncommon; it's a normal biological reaction and doesn't necessarily mean that sex is on the agenda. It can be affirming to feel that someone is attractive or attracted; acknowledge it and continue your conversation. If arousal persists (and it might on many occasions), it may be best if that part of the body is not in contact with the partner until calmer.[10]

If we're honest about human nature, some guys say they want to "cuddle" as a way to get sexual, so when I don't get sexual, some express disappointment, even anger. Vetting potential holding partners and sincere disclosure are important safeguards to avoiding problems. Sometimes you can tell with the first chat or photo whether a person is sincere about not being sexual with you. Seek God's guidance, too.

This discussion of boundaries for avoiding sexual relating brings us back to our friend, the libido. Historically, your default indicator of God-given same-sex needs may be your libido. The libido (even an erection or other physical signs of arousal) isn't a precise barometer of what exactly is going on inside you, of what really needs attention. I've found that my libido is ninety-five percent an emotional indicator, a rudimentary "check engine" light for multiple subtle social needs. These are core needs that we may have little experience identifying, let alone successfully meeting.[11]

If you respond to an insistent libido at face value, your focus will be on yourself and your desires—and the self is never satisfied in self-seeking. Sex isn't a need; sexual attempts to satisfy a demanding sex drive only make it more demanding, making you a servant to your libido's urges for ever more euphoric hits.

Real connection isn't about self but about relating with others. The next time your libido hollers for attention, rather than surrender to its in-your-face demands, ask yourself, "What's going on in my social world? Am I meeting my needs healthfully?"

If you're regularly meeting your emotional needs, you won't feel at war with your body—and you won't have to bottle up your feelings. The libido becomes very calm when emotional needs are met. Yes, I get erections—but I don't struggle with yearning; I bask in the affirming love that is filling me so overflowingly that I don't want for *anything* when embraces end (okay, perhaps a chocolate milkshake). This fulfillment lasts for days.

Intimacy can involve the senses and yet not be sexual. I find conversation, touch, emotional connection, and eye contact to be far greater and lasting than anything male-on-male sex offers. Is there thrill—even euphoria—in nonsexual holding? There is! Try it and observe how much better the relationship goes beyond touch.

If your libido is in the driver's seat rather than part of the instrument panel, or if you're steeped in delusions that same-sex sex is the best kind of connection or that the person you're with really wants sex even when they've said they don't, you're missing the point of human connection—and missing out on lasting union.

But what if you find yourself at the other end of the spectrum, craving connection but uncomfortable with physical touch or holding? There are a number of options in this chapter that don't involve touch but that build connection and intimacy. Affirming conversation is a supernal way to meet God-given emotional needs—even without holding. Any work or leisure activity can be a bonding experience.

C. S. Lewis said nonsexual ties are "as great a love as Eros. . . . Few value it because few experience it. And the possibility of going through life without the experience is rooted in the fact which separates [it] so sharply from . . . other loves. . . . [Familial] affection and [Romantic] Eros were too obviously connected with our nerves. . . . But in . . . that luminous, tranquil, rational world of relationships freely *chosen*—you got away from all that. This alone, of all the loves, seemed to raise you to the level of gods or angels."[12]

THREE KEYS

Some people say, "I've cuddled with my partner—but sex is better." However, they are speaking of sexual euphoria, which never lasts; the profound connection I'm talking about only comes with restraint—but not perpetually, because when true needs are met, urges are calmed. To understand its value, true union has to be experienced and might require not being sexual with anyone of one's sex.

Until you bond nonsexually, connection will not yield its best rewards. If you are easily distracted by visual stimuli or the quest for orgasm, it may take you longer to connect and come to value three keys to lasting same-sex fulfillment:

A. A personal understanding that your attraction to those of your own sex is part of God's plan for you (though a person might not presently understand the best way to express it; see chapter 3)
B. A personal belief that the most satisfying, longest-lasting same-sex bonding happens nonsexually and that orgasms with those of one's own sex are nowhere near as deep or lasting a bond (this is commonly grasped in the first embrace with no sexual agenda; *many* people experience this initially, then—thinking more is more—obliterate it via sex)
C. A personal realization that—good as they are—orgasms and sexual relating with those of one's own sex, regardless of deep emotion, diminish lasting union

Don't battle your libido; assuage it. Ideally, you will experience emotional fulfillment early and become certain of the other ideas soon thereafter. While I experienced profound connection in my first holding session, you might not. Perhaps you connect best via different activities or simple conversation. Consider that old ways of thinking or relating might be holding you back; then, allow yourself to let go of relating options that don't serve you. The more you *personally* comprehend—via experiencing superior satisfaction—that nonsexual connection is deeper and more lasing than same-sex sex (and that same-sex sex detracts from connection), the more you will treasure other kinds of relating over sexual activities with those of your sex. If you can't get to a place where you believe at least two of the above keys—if you keep same-sex sex as "plan B"—you might never attain lasting same-sex fulfillment.

> *"When we say no to something, we say yes to something else."*[13]
>
> —Ganel-Lyn Condie

It's not just your actions but also what's on your mind. Indulging in same-sex sexual thoughts or acts increases their hold on a person and diminishes the unique and profound union few know can exist. This happens because these individuals' focus on sex prevents the growth that leads to resilient connection.

It's a mistake to think sexual thoughts are harmless. They might be common, but untamed, they can be frustrating and counterproductive to lasting satisfaction. This may sound obvious (or perhaps impossible to some, at first), but try to avoid sexual thoughts and fantasies—even when not with your activity/conversation/holding partner. Don't try to simply manage these thoughts; I don't think I know a mortal capable of maintaining sexual thoughts or longing at a certain threshold. Surrender them entirely to God. This *is* doable, though it may take prayer and practice.[14]

For our own benefit, God prefers our honesty in prayer. Don't hesitate to confess to Him what He already knows. Maybe it's: "I think I want sex with this person, but I have a better, longer-lasting outcome in mind, if you will help me." Praying silently for blessings upon your pal also reduces selfish urges—though the best remedy is feeling pure love and fulfillment. Deep lasting connection takes more intention, but it yields superior rewards. Again, when my relationships fill the cup of my emotional need, sexual yearning is scarce; I feel more grounded and content overall.[15]

One surprising area of strength for me has come thanks to my addiction. Gay men in Utah are accustomed to arguing with people about Church chastity standards (no extramarital, nonmonogamous, or same-sex sex; see opening questions in chapters 1 and 5). Once people learn that my relationships today are more satisfying than past sexual ones, their standard arguments about repressive religion evaporate.[16]

Some still pressure me to be sexual "as long as there is no penetration," as though this arbitrary delineation of what constitutes sex does not alter the nature and outcome of the interaction. For me, penis stimulation takes my focus off my holding partner and onto myself; it *never* meets my same-sex emotional needs. Again, wanting more always leads to wanting more.

Sometimes I have to explain the hollowness and trauma of living under compulsion and being out of control; I rarely get pressured for sex after that. The part that some people have trouble understanding is that I genuinely feel a greater connection in nurturing interactions than I ever did when seeking to satisfy physical urges. My male relationships today surpass previous ones, but not in spite of abstinence; they are superior *because* they are not sexual. I cannot describe the complete contentment of loving and being loved by someone who loves me for who I am, who isn't using me in an attempt to pacify emotional needs via sex.

You may balk at this, but judge it on your own: In sexual relations with those of your sex, how much is the other person's whole being your *primary* concern? In nonsexual connecting, I usually bond because I feel genuine care and love—I want every good thing for the person I'm with.

In the first embrace with my asexual but affectionate friend Stan, he and I each experienced mind-expanding epiphanies. Halfway through our cuddle and conversation, I realized that Stan had made zero efforts to push my boundaries. Some guys, excited by the novelty of contact or curious whether I'm serious about boundaries, "accidentally" brush a hand on my groin or subtly grind their pelvis into me to see how or whether I'll respond. Stan hadn't attempted anything of the sort. It was then that I realized that asexuality is real.

About the same time, Stan happily realized, "Karl's not trying to have sex with me!" He told me that he had connected with approximately two hundred men, each proclaiming they only wanted to cuddle; I was the first whose actions backed up my words. I've since cuddled with other homoromantic asexual people (some have more rigid boundaries than mine); we all have similar needs.

As you realize your true needs are being met, bliss and generous feelings toward others can replace self-absorption, even addiction. When someone feels fulfilled, images, fantasies, and even outright propositions lose their allure. I no longer have to call a war council against lust. I cherish the deeper union I never found in the extremes of pretended independence or in detaching stimulation.

Nonsexual relating seems to be the ideal way for any two men or two women to meet true same-sex emotional needs. It's a paradox, but had Heavenly Father not led me to these bonds, my suppressed needs would likely have pulled me "off the wagon" again, in spite of—or due to—my previous isolating rules.

While I believe nonsexual same-sex relating is more profound than the average person ever experiences, some don't want the kind of interaction I describe, because not everyone is ready or willing to be vulnerable in this way—and not everyone experiences love via touch.[17] The me of thirty years ago might not have been able to stop at nonsexual holding (though I might have with a selfless guide). The me of even fifteen years ago would have run, afraid of my libido.

This is what works for me, but it's just one way. I *don't* encourage it for minors or for any two people who lack experience controlling their passions. Likewise, if you are a sex addict or a people pleaser, you must be hypervigilant in maintaining personal boundaries in order to experience true whole-soul connection. An independent accountability partner that you check in with before or after connecting can help you avoid complications. Friends who speak the truth; who probe your choices, fuzzy logic, or rationalizations; and who remind you of your goals and commitments are priceless!

Remember how I wrote that in the thick of my addiction, it seemed God was not hearing or helping me? Though I later discovered that grace has been extended to me every day, God has never, *ever* removed my need for emotional connection with men; this is because He gave me this need (just like He gave, and will never remove, my need for water until I die).

You may have found a different way to meet your emotional needs—shared interests and activities, service, giving, or simple conversations where validation abounds.[18] Whatever you do, don't ignore God-given needs—isolation is poison.

Regularly seek connection with others in healthful ways. Like oxygen, emotional fulfillment requires ongoing intake.[19] Tamping down or ignoring legitimate needs eventually fails. Long-suppressed needs find a way of expressing themselves, one way or another. Spencer W. Kimball said that "sin is the result of deep and unmet needs."[20]

HAPPY HOMME, HAPPY HOME; HAPPY HER, HAPPY SIR

Reed, a gay friend who has been married to a woman for decades, concluded that sex with guys wouldn't fulfill him. He shared these ideas with his wife—and she wholeheartedly encouraged him to associate with me and other men who also feel that touch and emotional connection are true needs and that sex disrupts same-sex bonding.[21]

Guys, you need buddies! If you're married, it's an excellent idea to discuss your connection objectives with your spouse, including buddy-vetting criteria and how things will be kept nonsexual (chapter 11 details how this can become a person's preferred way to interact over some herculean act of resistance. A person whose needs are being met has little interest in same-sex sexual relating). Ultimately, every spouse must let their partner move about freely, because restricting a partner's access to others makes the marriage vulnerable to infidelity and other ills.

I've mostly discussed men, but clearly, women should keep girlfriends who share their goals and values—doing so meets a God-given need! If married, encourage your man to have wholesome male friends. You will both feel more well-rounded and socially and emotionally healthy, and you'll experience greater harmony when together.

Have a spouse or a same-sex partner you want to keep? These principles will do more toward keeping you together and eliminating jealousy than anything I know. They may even remedy cheating, not least because emotional needs are not confused with sex. Moreover, the relationship between you won't tend to fizzle like ones based on sexual euphoria; it's that pleasure basis which motivates a person to constantly seek sexual satisfaction elsewhere since euphoria doesn't last.

WONDERFULLY MADE

I genuinely believe that resilient same-sex bonding is very likely when people stop seeking same-sex orgasm as a means of satisfying emotional needs; I've experienced the difference. If your relationship has been damaged by selfishness and pleasure-seeking, know that same-sex bonds can be repaired. Bear in mind, though, that your most rewarding relationships may not be the one(s) you're in, pursuing, or longing for. A change in what you seek or how you seek it could save you decades of frustration and heartbreak and fulfill you beyond your current expectations.[22]

While avoiding heartbreak isn't the top priority, consider that looking at same-sex relationships from a different perspective can facilitate more enduring, healthful connections, which has the added benefit of reduced heartbreaks. If you're aware your libido is a God-given (largely emotional) gauge, you can work with it rather than battling it, bottling it, or being its slave. Again, awareness of your options will empower you and increase satisfaction. Don't permit yourself to be driven by impulse—or to feel left out—for one more instant.

I present this not as a stopgap for people who wish to keep religious or other commitments—not as a way to *endure* temptation—but as a way to actually meet legitimate needs and enjoy ongoing fulfillment.

If you need a scriptural basis for any of this, consider again the deep affection between Christ and John the Beloved, or between King David and Jonathan, or among Apostles. I'd bet you know a heterosexual man who, if honest, will tell you of a special bond he shares with another man or men that is both profound and unique to what he shares with his wife or girlfriend.

God knows you, and He has always known what (and who!) would attract you. I'm convinced He knows you must bond with those of your sex to thrive. He also knows that "over"-connecting won't fill you the way circumscribed emotional connection does.[23] In all my sexual activity (even in exclusive relationships), I never once experienced deep, lasting connection with a man until I tried it with no sexual agenda. Discipline truly yields the greatest payoffs.

POINTS TO PONDER

- To relate with those of one's sex in a lasting, fulfilling way, a person must gain their *own* conviction (not mine, not your pastor's) of two or more of the following:
    A. Your attraction to those of your sex is part of God's plan for your happiness.
    B. Nonsexual same-sex connection fulfills best (leaving scarce room for lust).
    C. Same-sex sexual relations erode the bonding sought.

  You can work with your libido instead of battling it or being its slave. The libido becomes very calm when emotional needs are met. What have you observed about the ebb and flow of your own sex drive, and how is it affected by what's going on in the rest of your life?
- Same-sex sexual stimulation takes one's focus from the conversation/activity partner onto the self; it *never* meets same-sex emotional needs. The self is *never* satisfied. Naked holding or indulging in same-sex sexual thoughts also distract from true connection.
- Conversation is a super way to meet God-given emotional needs—even without embracing. In your own experience, what ways of relating have been effective in building and nurturing emotional bonds?

- Physical arousal is a normal biological reaction in human relating; it doesn't necessarily mean sex is on the agenda.
- Male-female relations have their unique perks. Few people have experienced the particular fulfillment only achieved with those of one's own sex. What distinct joys and benefits do you notice in your varied relationships?
- Nonsexual same-sex connecting is *not* a technique to endure temptation—it satisfies God-given needs, reduces frustration, and brings joyful relationships that can last forever.

NOTES

1. Marshal Burtcher (personal social media post, 2022).
2. Addicts know that eliminating something from one's life requires that it be replaced (hopefully with something more beneficial). If you simply stop something and don't start something positive in its place, you're likely to go back to previous habits. Matt. 12:43–45; Luke 11:24–26.
3. CuddleComfort.com (or search "ACE" or platonic groups. No site can guarantee that their members will behave in platonic ways).
4. See Vivian Manning-Schaffel, "The Health Benefits of Hugging," Better by Today, October 25, 2018, https://www.nbcnews.com/better/pop-culture/health-benefits-hugging-ncna920751; Ashley Uzer, "10 Health Benefits of Hugging, Backed by Science" MindBodyGreen, March 26, 2020, https://www.mindbodygreen.com/articles/

hugging-health-benefits; Francis McGlone and Susannah Walker, "Four Ways Hugs Are Good for your Health," *Greater Good Magazine*, June 22, 2021, https://greatergood.berkeley.edu/article/item/four_ways_hugs_are_good_for_your_health; Erica Cirino, "What Are the Benefits of Hugging?" Healthline, last updated April 11, 2018, https://www.healthline.com/health/hugging-benefits#1.-Hugs-reduce-stress-by-showing-your-support.

5. Same-sex public nudity (bathing) was once common and can be healthful (generally, society has sexualized even this, so boundaries are needed here too). Yet, I believe nudity and cuddling do not go well *together* and should be separate activities. "Eros will have naked bodies; friendship naked personalities." Lewis, *The Four Loves*, 71. Russ Peterson, "Inoculating Children Against Pornography" in *Faith in the Fire: An Outside Perspective on Latter-Day Families* (self-pub., Kindle Direct Publishing, 2021), Kindle.
6. See RiShawn Bittle, "How to Say No When it Counts," Full Focus, accessed August 21, 2022, https://fullfocus.co/say-no/.
7. Full body holding isn't necessarily unhealthy, but it can put one's focus on bodies rather than on soul connecting. Lingering on top of someone may be counterproductive in your goal to meet emotional needs and not be driven by physical urges. You'll need to understand yourself very well to be successful. If you desire to kiss, ask yourself: "Will kissing shift my focus away from healthfully meeting same-sex needs?" That's a personal question only you can answer.
8. While there might be natural consequences, God will not condemn you for breaking a bad commitment.

9. Some boundary guidance: Chantelle Pattemore, "How to Set Boundaries in Your Relationships," Psych Central (blog), June 3, 2021, https://psychcentral.com/blog/why-healthy-relationships-always-have-boundaries-how-to-set-boundaries-in-yours.
10. Our focus often determines our reality. Please see endnote 7 in chapter 4.
11. See Marc DiJulio, "Male Sexuality and Emotional Needs," Innovative Men's Health (blog), n.d., https://innovativemen.com/blog/male-sexuality-and-emotional-needs; Wikipedia, s.v. "Sexual desire," last modified August 10, 2022, 10:24, https://en.wikipedia.org/wiki/Sexual_desire.
12. Lewis, *The Four Loves*, 92, 67, 58–59, 72–73, emphasis added.
13. Ganel-Lyn Condie, *You Are More Than Enough—You Are Magnificent* (American Fork: Covenant Communications, 2018), 84. We would do well to forsake the "good" for the "better" or "best." Dallin H. Oaks, "Good, Better, Best," *Ensign*, November 2018, https://www.churchofjesuschrist.org/study/general-conference/2007/10/good-better-best?lang=eng.
14. On prayer: Russell M. Nelson, "Revelation for the Church."
15. A 24-hour technique addicts use that might enable a sex-focused person to attain appreciation for nonsexual connection is to say to sexual impulses, "Not today." James 4:7. "Lust only yields to the slow, patient working of the program" (or steps of surrender to God). *Sexaholics Anonymous* ("White Book"), 157. See also "Coming from AA, He Worked the Steps All Over Again in SA (Lawrence M., Virginia, USA),"

Sexaholics Anonymous, n.d., https://www.sa.org/essay/coming-from-aa-he-worked-the-steps-all-over-again-in-sa-lawrence-m-virginia-usa/.

16. "Sharing becomes a liberating and life giving experience." *Sexaholics Anonymous,* 87.
17. Gary Chapman, *The 5 Love Languages: The Secret to Love that Lasts* (Winston-Salem: Northfield Publishing, 2014).
18. Chapman, *The 5 Love Languages.*
19. Lewis, *The Four Loves*, 15
20. "Jesus saw sin as wrong but also was able to see sin as springing from deep and unmet needs on the part of the sinner." Spencer W. Kimball, "Jesus: The Perfect Leader," *Ensign*, August 1978.
21. 2 Ne. 9:51. While my libido remains strong, my urges for sex are barely noticeable because my real needs are emotional. Since establishing especially deep and lasting connections, I almost never experience an impulse to self-stimulate.
22. 1 Sam. 20:41–42; John 13:23, 19:25–27. See also Alma 53:2.
23. The following are musts for any successful friendship or relationship: honesty, accountability, forgiveness, love, respect, openness, loyalty, gentleness, acceptance, appreciation, trust, commitment, patience, recreation, sensitivity, and fascination. Of course, a person is most likely to find relationship happiness if they are already happy with self and with God. See Karl W. Beckstrand, *The Joys of Male Connection* (Midvale, UT: Paths Press, November 2022).

CHAPTER 11

The Key to Lasting Same-Sex Relationships

I have had a rich life of brothers. Men in my life that bless me in so many ways. Many of these brothers started out as a bromance. Meaning there was an attraction of some sort. Let's be real, attraction is one of the number one reasons we create friends in the first place. We are attracted to something about them. . . . I think bromances are healthy and wonderful. A bromance done right can . . . most often [turn] into a lifetime friendship.[1]

—*Brad Petersen*

AFTER THIS CHAPTER, I DON'T THINK you'll find it odd that I'm not into typical gay love stories and have no sexual or spousal designs on any man. (Again, please pardon the mostly male references; these are my experiences. I suspect much of what I say here also applies to women.)

My early relationships with men, like perhaps many of yours, didn't last long, even when we tried to make them last.

Knowing now how often sexual euphoria is confused with love and union, this doesn't surprise me. Today, I'm certain that, like the profound bonds some heterosexual men enjoy with each other, my current male (and female) relationships will continue to be close and rewarding in eternity.[2]

As I began to enjoy deep, lasting connection with men—eternal connections that God led me to—some guys inquired about becoming partners. It is understandable if a person's initial impulse in finding deep connection is to partner exclusively; the feelings of union can be solid and less likely to evaporate as they seem to when sexual climax is in the mix.

Exclusivity is fine, but sharing affection with multiple people may be more how your heart works toward those of your sex (and it has benefits). Remember that this type of bond does not presuppose complete fidelity or forsaking of other partners in the same way that marriage does. While I am not opposed to living with a like-minded man (someone who knows, as I do, that same-sex relationships last longer and are deeper when they are not sexual), I have encountered an unexpected dilemma: Some men wanting a live-together situation have wanted my heart *exclusively*, and I currently love *three* guys—deeply! My bonds with some men have endured for years.

ON JEALOUSY—A NEW MIND

You read that correctly: three. For a time, I felt like a freak among gay/bi men for loving more than one man.

Then, a friend asked me whether I felt jealous when one of these three "eternal soul brothers" spent time with—even held—another guy. My immediate and honest response was no.

I'd spoken that truth without thinking, so this was a mind-blowing revelation to *me*; it's what helped me grasp the secret of male relationships (though it shouldn't be a secret!—and it likely is the same among women). Not only are men capable of loving each other intensely and lastingly, as long as we don't try to fit into the male-female couple model, but also, there is no limit on how *many* soul brothers we can share profound love with—with no loss of love for anyone. And most men—straight or gay—are capable of great depth in most, if not all, of their same-sex relationships.

I wish I had a nickel for every gay husband who found himself attracted to a male guest at his own wedding. It's not because the newlywed is vile; he is simply a man—designed to love men (plural) deeply and uniquely from other kinds of love.

You may be content with having one "main squeeze"; just be aware of the nature of the male heart. Male love isn't a zero-sum thing (it's not a limited commodity that can run out). If you're ever drawn to a second man, it doesn't make you a reprobate, nor does it mean you love the first guy less; it may simply mean, unsurprisingly, that you're an ordinary man. You may already have found that you are capable of—or prone to—deep feelings for more than one guy. Honest heterosexual men will tell you this is normal. I'm persuaded that straight women likewise feel deep love for multiple women in their lives. Our Source of love is infinite![3]

You're not immoral for being drawn to more than one man—and you're not wicked if you have one guy who is special to you. You may be succeeding in pouring all of your guy love onto one partner. My perception of male love is that while that concentration *might* overwhelm an individual recipient, if there is overwhelm, it will most likely be within *you.* You may be bursting with feelings for other men, even ones you've just met (and perhaps beating yourself up over it). I suspect that love for people of our own sex is like fertilizer: most nurturing if spread broadly. Force it all into one spot, and you might kill the relationship.[4]

Again, having someone special is awesome; I *do* spend more time with one of my soul brothers than the others. He is happy to know that's the case, but he doesn't ask whether he's my favorite, and he doesn't worry when I spend time with someone else; this goes both ways. If your favorite guy isn't asking you for emotional exclusivity, don't take that chore upon yourself, even secretly (if he *is* asking it, you might consider carefully how healthful and doable such a request is for you).

Concentrating something that seems to be intended for broad distribution might incite needless jealousy, self-loathing, or discouragement. I don't discount special love between two people; remember too that same-sex bonds are different than opposite-sex bonds (I honestly feel they are deeper in many ways). If you're not sexual with your male circle, chances are that all such relations will be rewarding and lasting—you have discovered a key to long-term male love. How you interact with each person will, of course, vary (your feelings won't necessarily be equal for each guy).

Vern, a gay man in Salt Lake City, has had a boyfriend for many years. From what I understand, they are deeply committed to each other but are no longer sexual (by choice). This doesn't mean that they don't have social needs outside of their relationship. Vern sought my friendship as something safe because he felt that my lifestyle could never jeopardize his relationship with his boyfriend.

When we understand these deep bonds for what they are, neediness and jealousy fade. If you get a twinge of the green-eyed monster, as I thought I had a couple years ago, consider how much you might be being influenced by *romanticism*—the nonsensical dogma that persuades a person that a *true* love will know a person's unspoken thoughts and fulfill all needs or that sex equates to (or even trumps) unity. These ideas have harmed humanity in general for generations.[5] Overcoming our culture's harmful fixation on romance will help you to see your loved ones as they are and to love truly, deeply, and without jealousy. Indeed, C. S. Lewis described voluntary nonsexual relationships as "the least jealous of loves."[6]

If you examine your experiences with men, you may find, like I did, that what men sometimes mistake for a partner-type jealousy is actually a generalized buddy jealousy.[7] Think about it: Someone you love gives a hug to someone else; are you feeling hatred for the "competition" for taking up all your guy's love (impossible, because it isn't finite)—or do you wish this special guy showed you love in the same *way* they show it to the other person? It doesn't mean your important guy doesn't love you! It may just be that they don't love you as deeply or spend as much time with you as you wish. This is a normal aspect of human relationships (people can be jealous of others' jobs, hobbies, or even religious practices because they take a special person's attention away).

My sense is that what some might refer to as emotional infidelity is impossible among people of the same sex. If we understand and accept that the male heart (heterosexual or gay) naturally tends toward deep love for multiple people of our sex, we won't worry much whether someone loves us as much or in the same way as they love someone else. We also won't have doubts about our own lack of commitment to a special guy when we experience emotional connections with other guys, and we won't feel possessive or afraid that our soul brother(s) might emotionally "cheat." We'll actually be okay with an intimate brother loving other men because we understand the natural workings of the human heart toward those of one's own sex.

Tad, a gay man who respects my boundaries, grasps that loving one man doesn't mean love can't exist with other men. While we share a deep closeness, neither of us feels possessive of the other, and each of us are close to other men.

If you see me with my arm around a guy, I'm not signaling ownership or marking turf. The men in my life are not possessions; you are welcome to love them too. If you see me being affectionate with a guy, I hope it's an indicator that you can receive pure affection from me and, most importantly, that *you* can share healthful male affection with other men.

While I may tell a soul brother that I love him, each of us must comprehend that I am capable of feeling the same for other people simultaneously—and so is he![8] It is a gift to feel deep love for multiple people and recognize that it in no way diminishes the intensity of love that we two share. This depth, clarity, and freedom is directly connected to nonsexual relating.

A NEW APPRECIATION FOR THE MERITS OF CHASTITY

It's liberating and healthful to discover the profound connection that's unique to people of the same sex, to understand that no eternal soul brother or soul sister relationship suffers for not conforming to the heterosexual couple model. Rather than compare the standards of chastity and fidelity in opposite-sex marriage to parameters for other kinds of relationships, it's simplest to recognize that heterosexual love and same-sex love are *not* competing loves; each is unique. There are infinite ways to love because there are multiple kinds of relationships—God created them!

Here's the best news of all, especially to those who've seen a lack of fidelity among men who are sexual with men: Because the general nature of male love isn't exclusive—and if you keep from mentally associating love with sexual euphoria—you're much less likely to fall out of "love" with a man you now love, even if you acknowledge love for another man.[9] Without this insight—that is, while seeking pleasure (or evading heartbreak)—a person is more likely to abandon one man after another. It's like gorging on empty calories and remaining hungry rather than feasting on the nourishment that is same-sex emotional bonding.

I'm *not* preaching gay polyamory, because I'm not endorsing gay sex, much less with multiple partners. Yes, sexual euphoria is exhilarating, but nonsexual connection is *more* fulfilling and resilient (yet still euphoric)! Love and sex do not always go well together. Unfortunately, some have seen their love damaged or destroyed when sexual appetite overpowers consideration of another's comfort or even consent. Such selfishness runs counter to true connection, and sex in these circumstances not only fails to meet legitimate emotional needs of the soul but also might deepen the yearning. By neglecting true emotional connection, the feeling of neediness persists, regardless of how much sex one has.[10]

My gay friend Lucas summed it up: "Once the high of wanting someone so intensely is recognized—not as love, but as euphoria inside the self—one can look toward the *other* man's happiness. And that joint happiness doesn't seem to involve orgasms." In other words, it's focusing on someone else's happiness that really feeds us. "'We all think we want to be loved, but what actually feels good to us is feeling loving,' clinical psychologist Lisa Firestone, Ph.D., tells *The Huffington Post*. . . . 'When we have feelings of caring or love for other people, we feel better.'"[11]

People in the Bible were first commanded to love their neighbors as themselves.[12] Christ took it a step further: "Love one another as *I* have loved you." Love is a verb; it is a focus of attention on the other rather than the self. It involves seeing people as they are. To love as Christ loved involves giving of self with no thought of receiving. When we can do this, we will burst into a new level of consciousness, relating, and joy—and these things can be shared epiphanies beyond what we've previously experienced.[13]

It can be difficult to grasp and accept this ideal of love, especially if you've been living with a different set of assumptions for a long time. As we're patient with ourselves and each other, we can see this selfless love have a positive impact in our lives.

John is a dear friend of multiple years who lives with a boyfriend who is not affectionate. They rarely have sex anymore. John really appreciates that I express love via touch, but he would often ask me for sex. I explained that the reason he and I are so close is *because* we're not sexual. One day, John stormed out of my place—determined not to return. "You're not giving me what I want," he said. "I guess I'll have to find it elsewhere."

Two or three days later, John came back. "I miss the emotion we share," he said. The kind of union John and I have isn't found in male-on-male sex. Still, he struggled to let go of the belief that mutual sexual ecstasy with me would only make our connection better. He fantasized about it and would occasionally masturbate when visiting me, when I wasn't in the room with him. After some weeks, he stopped. When we talked about it, he said our connection was better and longer lasting when he didn't masturbate. On days when he had masturbated, he soon wanted to leave; now, when he's here, he's reluctant to leave. He discovered this all on his own, and our friendship is better for it. I am not jealous of John's boyfriend, and John is not jealous of the other friends I share affection with.

When I contrast my past sexual relationships with the profound and lasting intimacy I now enjoy, there is simply no comparison.[14] Far from practicing a grudging, hair-shirt celibacy, I gladly abstain from sex because I refuse to sacrifice my deep, affectionate bonds to return to shallow, distancing same-sex sex.

If I seem unromantic to you because I'm not drawn to gay love stories, understand it's because they fail to do justice to limitless and profound same-sex love—and because they seem deceptive regarding the resiliency of sexual same-sex partnerships (also because my life is filled with real, *lasting* relationships).

POINTS TO PONDER

- Most people prefer loving to being loved; it is a gift to feel deep love for others, including those of one's sex. Truly loving relationships can continue in eternity. How have different types of love fulfilled you in different ways?
- Heterosexual love and same-sex love are *not* competing loves; each is unique, and all people are designed to love those of their own sex richly. Our Source of love is infinite!
- Because nonsexual same-sex love isn't necessarily exclusive—and helps us not confuse love with sexual euphoria—falling "out of love" isn't common. How are you liberated in knowing you can share deep same-sex bonds with more than one "soul brother" or "soul sister"?
- There is an inverse relationship between the selfish pursuit of sexual gratification and the ability to engage in genuine, fulfilling sex-same emotional connections, with the latter more consistently offering durable fulfillment than the former. Does my observation surprise you? How have you seen this interplay at work in your own life?

NOTES

1. Chef Brad, Facebook, winter 2022, https://www.facebook.com/profile.php?id=754211589.

2. "And that same sociality which exists among us here will exist among us [in Heaven], only it will be coupled with eternal glory." D&C 130:2; Moses 7:63.
3. Eph. 3:17–19.
4. "Putting the weight of all our deepest hopes and longings on the person we 'love' will crush him or her with our expectations." Timothy Keller, Facebook, spring 2022, https://www.facebook.com/TimKellerNYC.
5. See Ty Mansfield (quoting Robert Millet on theological [and cultural] viruses), "Balancing the Tensions of Our Latter-day Saint and LGBTQ Conversations," *Deseret News*, October 21, 2021, https://www.deseret.com/opinion/2021/10/21/22717022/balancing-the-tensions-of-our-latter-day-saint-and-lgbtq-conversations-mormon-truth-love. See also The School of Life, "How Romanticism Ruined Love," YouTube video, May 30, 2016, https://www.youtube.com/watch?v=jltM5qYn25w; Mark Manson, "A Brief History of Romantic Love and Why It Kind of Sucks," Mark Manson: Life Advice That Doesn't Suck (blog), n.d., https://markmanson.net/romantic-love; and Mark Manson, "Romance Is Like Alcohol," Mark Manson: Life Advice That Doesn't Suck (blog), n.d., https://markmanson.net/romance.
6. Nonsexual "love, free from instinct, free from all duties but those which love has freely assumed, almost wholly free from jealousy, and free without qualification from the need to be needed, is eminently spiritual. It. . . . is the sort of love one can imagine between angels. Have we found the natural love which is Love itself?" Lewis, *The Four Loves*, 61, 77.
7. Lewis, 57.

8. I have held women, heterosexual and gay men, asexuals, and a transgendered person—each has been satisfying.
9. Life coach Brad Petersen says boyfriends get jealous and possessive; brothers don't:

   > Another falsehood is . . . I am told that my love has limits, "Only so much to go around." If I were looking for [a boyfriend] perhaps that might be true, but in the search for brothers I have learned this very important lesson: The human heart, my heart and your heart, has an unlimited capacity to love as many as deeply as we want. There are no limits to the amount of brothers one can love and enjoy. . . . The more I love the greater my heart expands. After all we are created in God's image and Christ is our example in all things. His love knew and knows no limits. It is limitless. We have the same gift as Christ has: To love as many as deeply as we want, in other words, why limit how [deeply/many] we love? . . . "I don't need a boyfriend, I need brothers that respect me and help me to be closer to Christ, my dearest brother. I need men that love deeply and are aware, in the process, we . . . have to come to understand and control our mortal bodies." Chef Brad, Facebook, winter 2022.

10. See Jett Stone, "Why Men Need to Prioritize, and Celebrate, Their Friendships," Psychology Today (blog), February 8, 2022, https://www.psychologytoday.com/us/blog/the-souls-men/202202/why-men-need-prioritize-and-celebrate-their-friendships.
11. Lindsay Holmes, "8 Ways to Tell if You're a Truly Compassionate Person," *Huffington Post*, last updated December

7, 2017, emphasis added, https://www.huffingtonpost.co.uk/entry/habits-of-compassionate-people_n_5522941.

12. Mark 12:31.
13. John 15:12–13.
14. John 13:34. "Love is what you've been through with somebody." James Thurber, James Thurber Quotes. BrainyQuote.com, BrainyMedia Inc, accessed August 17, 2022, https://www.brainyquote.com/quotes/james_thurber_106549.

CHAPTER 12

Authentic Identity—The Key to Happiness

Sexuality may operate without Eros [love] or as part of Eros. . . . I make the distinction…to limit our inquiry and without any moral implications. I am not at all subscribing to the popular idea that it is the absence or presence of [love] which makes the sexual act "impure" or "pure," degraded or fine, lawful or unlawful. If all who lay together without being in the state of [love] were abominable, we all come of tainted stock[!] The times and places in which marriage depends on Eros are in a small minority. Most of our ancestors were married off in early youth to partners chosen by their parents on grounds that had nothing to do with [love]. . . . And they did [fine]. . . . Conversely, this [sexual] act, done under the influence of a soaring and iridescent [Romantic love] which reduces the role of the [mind] to a minor consideration, may yet be plain adultery, may involve breaking a wife's heart, deceiving a husband, betraying a friend, polluting hospitality and deserting your children. It has not pleased God that the distinction between a sin and a duty should turn on fine feelings. This act, like any other, is justified (or not) by far more prosaic and definable criteria; by the keeping or breaking of promises, by justice or injustice, by charity or selfishness."[1]

—*C. S. Lewis*

IS GOD THE SOURCE OF TRAUMA?

CONSIDER THE INCLINATION TO BASE OUR decision-making on our feelings or sensations: A "good" decision is, ostensibly, one that makes us feel good, or at least avoids feeling bad. However, some "negative" emotions come from within us and have a positive purpose: Fear can preserve life and protect us from harm; anger can help us preserve justice; grief can help us love better and be less selfish; guilt can help us be more careful with people's things and feelings and reconcile with God's wishes.[2]

Perhaps you have experienced what I have on occasion: acting sexually with someone you "shouldn't" and not feeling bad at all. You might go years without feeling any remorse or emptiness, as predicted by your elders.

I've learned that the voices of priests, parents, and peers can be silenced or avoided and that we can believe we have banished guilt. But God loves you too much to mute your internal compass forever.

One day, in this life or the next, you'll likely know for yourself that sex without God's blessing limits your joy. Regret may come to those who've done things out of order or with someone whom they were intended to love differently. This feeling won't be imposed on you or me externally; on our own, we'll come to recognize and value things that, currently, we might not.[3] I am *not* saying a person will be in hell with no way out! Members of The Church of Jesus Christ of Latter-day Saints don't believe in a permanent hell, except maybe for a small number of individuals who don't want any part of God's glory. Even damnation seems to have limits.[4]

Something a counselor shared with me applies both to lack of remorse and to self-loathing: Feelings by themselves are not the best gauge of personal progress toward happiness and are an incomplete basis for choices. Facts provide better data and should hold most of our attention. Regardless of current feelings, if God says sexual activity outside of respectful opposite-sex marriage is harmful, and you've been sexual outside of that, then a course change is advisable. My own pivots—which involve subordinating feelings to facts—have left my mind clearer and my heart lighter and open to more profound ideas and bonding.

On the other hand, being attracted to someone of your sex is *not* something to feel bad about.[5] Have a crush on someone who is taken or who could never be your spouse? That's a tough spot to be in, but it's not necessarily sin (though an obsession could get between you and God). While feelings can seem to have a will of their own, when coupled with facts, they can help us know what is best.[6]

> *"You can't shame or hate yourself into lasting change."*[7]
>
> —Scott Cone

Conscience—what the scriptures call the light of Christ—can help us avoid destructive behaviors. Guilt may *feel* bad, but it is a gift, a temporary prompt to correct something for our own happiness. Shame, on the other hand, is what the devil concocts out of ignored guilt or out of societal pressure. Shame is destructive and should be rejected.[8]

You may ask, "What if I still feel the Holy Spirit even though I've messed up?" The facts are that God loves you and that every man and woman has sinned. You are His child; nothing changes that. Your worth is immeasurable! People without the gift of the Holy Spirit may still feel His influence (or no one would come to know Christ). What we most need in this challenging life is the constant guidance of the Holy Spirit that comes from sincere, ongoing steps to follow Christ (see chapters 5 and 13). Trying counts with God.[9]

Understanding the positive roles of "negative" emotions can allow us to embrace them for personal development. These feelings become our constructive servants rather than tyrannical masters, another proof that there is a wise and loving God!

Maria Shanley says, "Authenticity is a highly specific, constantly changing state. You have to live it, be it, make mistakes, admit them, learn from them, and therein inspire others to find it within themselves." [10]

As a child of God, seeing and accepting yourself as you really are is essential. God accepts and loves you right now as you are. Does that mean He's completely satisfied with your development, that you need no more progress to be eternally happy? If you think about it, we absolutely need to acquire the moral qualities God has. Consider that He wants us all to eventually become like Him, which means acquiring purity, wisdom, and perfection, or we can't bear

His glory or even shoulder omniscience. (Again, the power to become omniscient and omnipotent is not ours, but the choice to receive that metamorphosis via Christ is entirely our decision).[11]

Coming out of the closet can be freeing and can lift your hopes. Refusing to be ashamed of who you are or what you feel is a great step forward! I encourage you to love yourself for who you are right now, remembering your divine origins. The danger is in believing that *all* enticements are worth pursuing or that the idea of self-discipline for higher goals comes from culture or church or a condemning god. Labeling rules as burdensome and rejecting them all is simplistic and risky.[12]

There are many dangers in indulging every appetite. In the case of sexual activity with few restraints, it can be addictive. Just as I did, you may find yourself going where you don't want to go and doing things you don't want to do with people you don't want to be with, ultimately becoming who you don't want to be. What some call "freedom" to be "authentic" can quickly morph into actual slavery to lust.[13]

It's a paradox: The surest way to *reduce* options is to reject any and all constraints, leaving no option off-limits. Often, rather than the desired pleasure being our servant, *we* become controlled by the thing we focus on. Freedom and opportunity are increased by the application of laws and boundaries. (A person who can't acknowledge equal and opposite reactions in everything will likely struggle to understand this.)[14]

Likewise, some people see faith as restraining, yet Christ is the only one who can free us from bondage. Making Him a part of your life is the only guarantee of ongoing liberty.[15]

Some people would rather carry shame than confess weakness—which we all have. Some would rather pretend they've done no wrong or that right and wrong, offense and harm are social constructs. Is that truly liberation, or is it bondage?[16]

I submit to you that it *is* a lie to pretend you're heterosexual if you're not. Like other lies, it can be harmful to others and to yourself. Living a lie can be remedied by embracing who you are *and* by embracing all that God promises you can become—starting now—with grace.[17] Pretending that no one is being hurt by abandoned standards or by redefining "harm" doesn't change facts; the destructive outcomes are overwhelmingly visible.[18]

Clearly, I'm not saying people must remain in miserable relationships. There are active and reflective methods to improving your situation from where you stand right now. Seek to resolve your relationships, and if necessary, end them with heaven's guidance; don't cheat and pretend it's not wrong or harmful. Don't be surprised if problems follow you once you're divorced, single, or in a new relationship; remember that dissatisfaction isn't always caused by spouse or family or church. Chapters 10 and 11 have options (things arguably better than isolating sex) that can enable a married or single person to feel fulfilled, honor their vows, and not abandon or traumatize family needlessly.

PERHAPS YOU DON'T NEED WHAT YOU THINK YOU NEED

Many people view chastity as a lot of "don'ts." Many Christians believe it is about one enormous Do, or more specifically, See! See people "as they really are."[19]

Eleanor Cain Adams and Allisa White write, "Chastity requires making a conscious choice to respect and regard others as divine beings. Simply believing we're respectful in our relationships isn't enough. . . . Do our acts demonstrate an understanding that we—and everyone else is—a literal spirit child of God? . . . David A. Bednar . . . taught that 'Intimate relations are one of the ultimate expressions of our divine nature.' Being chaste deepens love (and happiness) throughout eternity."[20]

On the path of recovery, celibacy and sobriety do not necessarily mean healthful or fulfilled. Celibacy may be considered chastity, but chastity is not celibacy; a person can be sexual *and* chaste, and a person can be celibate in their actions yet unchaste in their motivations and desires.

Emily Madsen Reynolds writes, "If we speak of sexuality as a gift replete with possibilities and bound by covenants . . . chastity doesn't end when sexual relations begin. In fact, it never ends. It is [an ideal path] to understand and engage human sexuality as a participant in [God's] Plan of [Happiness]."[21]

Embracing the *world's* version of being one's true self often means selfishness and disconnection from true union. This need not be permanent, but it can be difficult to understand—and escape (perhaps less easy than breaking a sex addiction).

Real authenticity, then, is being true to the divine in all of us. It's *in*authentic to pretend you are just an organism with only impulse for motivation rather than a child of God with the powerful gift of agency—to act with no requirement to be acted on, by impulse or anything else—if we continually look to the Great Liberator.[22] He's put no limit on the number of do-overs extended to us.[23]

Remember that my counselor told me it's normal for most people to have conflicting desires? (Examples: sleep versus stay up; bless others versus please self.) The best example might be the nearly universal desire to occasionally be away from people—yet be connected and a part of humanity at the same time.

If you think you can't live without sex, try going without and see (most people will likely be without a sexual partner at some point in life). Ask God's help; honest prayer includes acknowledging that we sometimes want what may not be best for us. If you don't want a heterosexual relationship, you don't have to have one (ever). If you're not sure you want sex, hold off for today; sex that you don't really want erodes intimacy. The connection almost all of us crave is jeopardized by self-centered sex that opens the spirit to negative influences. Conversely, by choosing selflessness and sincere living, you can create connections far deeper than sexual ones—now, in this life—as an LGBTQIA person. You don't have to wait until heaven to find that joy.[24]

God wants *us* to see how we'll choose—even in complex scenarios like love—but His way doesn't demand the sacrifice of *healthful* social connections, including with those of our own sex, because they are God-given (see other kinds of relationships in chapter 8). Peace depends on making choices (ultimately) like God would make, not because He says so, but because we have discovered that His way is the happy way, now and in the long term.[25] Again, God will never force us.

GOD NEED

"Theologians have often feared, in . . . love, a danger of idolatry. I think they meant by this that lovers might idolize one another. That does not seem to me to be the real danger; certainly not in marriage. . . . Even in courtship I question whether anyone who has felt the thirst for the Uncreated . . . ever supposed that the [b]eloved could satisfy it. . . . The real danger seems to me not that the lovers will idolize each other but that they will idolize Eros himself."[26]

Do you have a deep sense of lack in your life, something that nothing seems to satisfy? I've talked at length about social and emotional need, but we have other needs as well. It may be a hole that nothing on earth can fill; it may be a deep longing for your Father in Heaven. While social needs must be met by other human beings, your God need is also real. Just as God will not fill our human needs, humans cannot fill our God need. Regular worship in temple, church, mosque, or synagogue can help fill this need. While a person can call upon God and read His words anywhere, doing so with others has significant impact on our faith and hope.[27]

No matter how you feel, the fact is that God loves and wants you. The exhilaration of knowing you're attracted to your own sex and that God loves you *now* is real. However, love is not an excusal from God's commandments. His love is exalting and prompts us to use our agency to improve our choices, to stretch to be like Him. He will not lower His standards for our temporary comfort, because His love means He wants us to have all options, ability, and joy.

POINTS TO PONDER

- All emotions can enlighten us: Guilt moves us to repentance and helps us maintain relationships, freedom, and growth. Shame, by contrast, hinders growth and distancing us from God. How can you discern whether you're feeling guilt or shame?
- The surest way to reduce options is to reject constraints. Principles and boundaries can *increase* options (having or getting all you want can lead to bondage). How have you seen this paradox at work in your life?
- Because they're based on deprivation and denial, celibacy and sobriety don't necessarily mean healthful or whole. A person can be sexual and chaste, and a person can be celibate yet unchaste.

- God wants *us* to see what we'll choose—even in complex scenarios like human attachments. Are you ever surprised by your choices, and what do you learn when that happens?
- No mortal can meet all your needs. Intimacy can't be attained if one is out of sync with self or with God. Your God-need is legitimate as well. What options do you have for bringing God into your life more fully?

NOTES

1. Lewis, *The Four Loves*, 92.
2. Russ Peterson, *The Technology of Survival* (not yet published).
3. "To any who are tempted to walk or talk or behave in these ways—'as the world giveth' . . . don't expect it to lead to peaceful experience; I promise you in the name of the Lord that it won't." Jeffrey R. Holland, "Not as the World Giveth," *Ensign*, May 2021, https://www.churchofjesuschrist.org/study/general-conference/2021/04/23holland?lang=eng. See also Hel. 13:38; Alma 41:10, 42:25–30.
4. According to D&C 19:6–12, *Endless* and *Eternal* are appellations, applied to anything originating from our Eternal Father. We now know that all but a handful who do not want it will be saved forever in a kingdom of glory. "In my Father's house are many mansions." John 14:2. See D&C 19:4–13; D&C 76; Bible Dictionary, "Hell"; Bible Dictionary, "Damnation." Even those who don't want God's glory may not suffer torment forever: "Anglican church leader and academically credentialed classical scholar, Frederic W. Farrar,

who wrote *The Life of Christ*, asserted that the definition of [eternal] damnation in the King James Version of the Bible was the result of translation errors from Hebrew and Greek to English." Quentin L. Cook, "Conversion to the Will of God," *Liahona*, May 2022, https://www.churchofjesuschrist.org/study/general-conference/2022/04/29cook?lang=eng; Frederic W. Farrar, *Eternal Hope*, (New York: E. P. Dutton & Co., 1877) xiv–xv, xxxiv, 93; see also Appendix E (https://PremioBooks.com/joy or final page QR code).

5. Neither the scriptures nor The Church of Jesus Christ of Latter-day Saints condemn same-sex love (it's a gift), only sexual relationships between anyone not in wife-husband marriage.
6. "Feelings . . . are part of our God-given nature and serve a useful purpose. . . . We don't feel ashamed or guilty for feeling hungry!" "Fostering a Positive Perspective of Sexuality," *Ensign*, August 2020, 72, https://www.churchofjesuschrist.org/study/ensign/2020/08/young-adults/fostering-a-positive-perspective-of-sexuality?lang=eng.
7. Scott Cone (personal social media post, 2022).
8. See McKell A. Jorgensen, "Shame versus Guilt: Help for Discerning God's Voice from Satan's Lies," *Ensign*, January 2020, https://www.churchofjesuschrist.org/study/ensign/2020/01/young-adults/shame-versus-guilt-help-for-discerning-gods-voice-from-satans-lies?lang=eng; Wendy Ulrich, "3 Ways to Combat Shame and the Difference between Guilt and Shame and Why It Matters," *LDS Living*, December 27, 2018, https://www.ldsliving.com/3-ways-to-combat-shame-the-difference-between-guilt-and-shame-and-why-it-matters/s/89594.

9. "With the gift of the Atonement of Jesus Christ and the strength of heaven to help us, we can improve, and the great thing about the gospel is we get credit for trying, even if we don't always succeed." Jeffrey R. Holland, "Tomorrow the Lord Will Do Wonders Among You," *Ensign*, May 2016, https://www.churchofjesuschrist.org/study/general-conference/2016/04/tomorrow-the-lord-will-do-wonders-among-you?lang=eng.
10. Maria Shanley, "Learning What Authenticity Means to You," LinkedIn Pulse, April 1, 2022, https://www.linkedin.com/pulse/what-authenticity-means-you-maria-marie-shanley/?trackingId=L14Kl5jfQuu5YE7wVHLiiQ%3D%3D.
11. 2 Cor. 4:17. God's presence can't be endured if we don't resonate at His frequency of light and love (i.e., we must change and become in sync with Him). For Christ to fulfill His divine mission on earth, He absolutely had to know 100 percent who He was.
12. Von Keetch traveled to a bay in Australia renowned for its surfing. He met some American surfers who were upset that a heavy mesh barrier had been stretched across the mouth of the bay, right where the best waves were breaking. According to the surfers, the barrier went all the way to the ocean floor, ruining their "once-in-a-lifetime" surfing trip. An older, local man had them each look through his binoculars. What they saw were the dorsal fins of large sharks feeding near the reef on the other side of the barrier. "The old surfer . . . said: 'Don't be too critical of the barrier. . . . It's the only thing that's keeping you from being devoured.' Our perspective . . . changed. A barrier that had seemed . . . to curtail the fun and excitement . . . had become

. . . protection. . . . God's commands and standards . . . can sometimes be difficult to understand. . . . We often cannot comprehend the great dangers hidden . . . below the surface. But He who 'comprehends all things' knows exactly where those dangers lie. He gives us . . . loving guidance, so that we may avoid [much pain]." Von G. Keetch, "Blessed and Happy Are Those Who Keep the Commandments of God," *Ensign*, October 2015, https://www.churchofjesuschrist.org/media/video/2016-09-0009-blessed-and-happy-are-those-who-keep-the-commandments-of-god?lang=eng.

13. Please allow my experiences (and those you've observed around you) to serve in place of any you might not yet have, and let my cautionary example help you have increased options via positive choices.
14. See Helen Yu and Alison Guernsey, "What is the Rule of Law?" Freedom School, last updated February 22, 2022, https://freedom-school.com/law/what-is-the-rule-of-law.html.
15. Mos. 7:33; 2 Ne. 26:22, 28:22. See Dan Peterson, "Is Morality Merely an Illusion?" Sic et Non (blog), Patheos, August 14, 2022, https://www.patheos.com/blogs/danpeterson/2019/07/is-morality-merely-an-illusion.html?utm_medium=social&utm_source=share_bar#Yd-8jylqXChXQHPCB.01.
16. Matt. 15:19; 2 Peter 2:14, 18–19. How long can a relativist retain values if everything is equally valueless to them? I've seen trust and families crushed by people who claim they are simply being authentic or honest. Yes, life inflicts enormous pressures, but can a person be satisfied with the response, "It was either them or me"? *That idea comes from limited either/or thinking.*

17. "Coming out" may be only with oneself (whom one is attracted to is not everyone's business). "A man who lies to himself, and believes his own lies becomes unable to recognize truth, either in himself or in anyone else, and he ends up losing respect for himself and for others. When he has no respect for anyone, he can no longer love, and, in order to divert himself, having no love in him, he yields to his impulses, indulges in the lowest forms of pleasure, and behaves in the end like an animal. And it all comes from lying—lying to others and to yourself." Fyodor Dostoevsky, AZQuotes, AZQuotes.com, 2022, accessed August 17, 2022, https://www.azquotes.com/quote/588022.
18. See Nicole Howell, "A Link Between Single Parent Families and Crime (PhD diss., Olivet Nazarene University, 2015), https://digitalcommons.olivet.edu/cgi/viewcontent.cgi?article=1078&context=edd_diss; Vanessa Hemovich and William D. Crano, "Family Structure and Adolescent Drug Use: An Exploration of Single-Parent Families," *Substance Use & Misuse* 44, no. 14 (December 14, 2009), https://doi.org/10.3109/10826080902858375; R. L. Maginnis, "Single-Parent Families Cause Juvenile Crime" in *Juvenile Crime: Opposing Viewpoints* (Farmington Hills, MI: Greenhaven Press, 1997), 62–66, https://www.ojp.gov/ncjrs/virtual-library/abstracts/single-parent-families-cause-juvenile-crime-juvenile-crime-opposing; Kay Hymowitz, "The Real, Complex Connection between Single-Parent Families and Crime," *The Atlantic*, December 3, 2012, https://www.theatlantic.com/sexes/archive/2012/12/the-real-complex-connection-between-single-parent-families-and-crime/265860/; "Effects of Fatherless Families on

Crime Rates," MARRIpedia, n.d., http://marripedia.org/effects_of_fatherless_families_on_crime_rates. For more information on societal disintegration via non-God-approved sex (individual and societal), see Kirk Durston, "Why Sexual Morality May Be Far More Important Than You Ever Thought," Thoughts About God, Truth, and Beauty (blog), n.d., https://www.kirkdurston.com/blog/unwin.

19. Jac. 4:13.
20. Eph. 5:25. Eleanor Cain Adams and Allisa White, "Living the Law of Chastity in a Dating World Full of Gray Areas," *Ensign*, August 2020, https://www.churchofjesuschrist.org/study/ensign/2020/08/young-adults/living-the-law-of-chastity-in-a-dating-world-full-of-gray-areas?lang=eng; David A. Bednar, "We Believe in Being Chaste," *Ensign*, May 2013, 42. Note how Alma indicates to his son that charity (pure love) may *require* [purity]: "Bridle all your passions, that ye may be filled with love." Alma 38:12. See also Juli Slattery, *God, Sex, and Your Marriage* (Chicago: Moody Publishers, 2022).
21. Emily Madsen Reynolds, "Virtue and Abundant Life," *BYU Magazine*, Summer 2011, 47, https://magazine-dev.byu.edu/article/virtue-abundant-life/.
22. The human race (male and female)—is more than the instincts and appetites accorded it by nature. . . . [a prophet has said]: "God . . . hath created all things . . . both things to act and things to be acted upon" (2 Ne. 2:14). In teaching the seriousness of [sexual] sins, Alma also made certain his son understood that a person's actions have . . . impact on others as well: "Suffer . . . not the devil to lead away your heart again after . . . harlots. Behold, O my son, how great

iniquity ye brought upon the Zoramites; for when they saw your conduct they would not believe in my words" (Alma 39:11). Perhaps . . . some . . . [try] to minimize the damage . . . sin would cause [via] . . . the frequently used . . . excuse, "It's okay for me to sin. . . . It's my life, and I'm hurting only myself." . . . When individuals use their agency in such a way as to place their [glory] in jeopardy, [those closest to them] are affected by those choices. Sin of any kind—especially immorality—has serious consequences not only for ourselves but also for others." Terry B. Ball, "Alma 39: A Model for Teaching Morality," *The Religious Educator* 2, no. 2 (2001), https://rsc.byu.edu/vol-2-no-2-2001/alma-39-model-teaching-morality.

23. Mos. 26:30. "Though your sins be as scarlet, they shall be as white as snow," Isa. 1:18. "And thou wilt cast all their sins into the depths of the sea." Micah 7:19. "Thou art angry, O Lord, with this people, because they will not understand thy mercies which thou hast bestowed upon them because of thy Son." Alma 33:16. See Mos. 7:33; 2 Ne. 26:22, 28:22.
24. 2 Cor. 5:17.
25. Job 28:28.
26. Lewis, *The Four Loves*, 111, 128.
27. Eph. 4:11–14. See also "The Articles of Faith," Article 11.

CHAPTER 13

How to Not Miss Out—Covenants & Grace

"Don't lose faith in yourself. Faith in God means faith in His creation of you. He knew what He was doing. You are enough. You are incredible. You have what it takes to [become like Him]." [1]

—Hank Smith

POWERLESS—YET WITH MORE THAN TWO CHOICES IN MOST THINGS

WHAT IF YOUR CHALLENGE ISN'T IN acknowledging natural and moral law? What if your challenge is feeling *incapable* of living it? As an addict, I know that feeling intimately; it can be completely disheartening![2]

It is okay to feel like you can't toe the line or meet God's expectations—because on your own, you can't! That's what we are born to learn: While we may or may not be stronger than mortal nature or Satan on any given day, our Savior is forever flawless and omnipotent; He can become the personal perfection that we lack.

Mortal voices can muddle what God asks of us; Satan can make us feel that God's path is too difficult or that God doesn't want us because we have flaws (how logical is the idea that we have to be clean before coming to the cleanser of sins?). If discouragement doesn't work, Satan will try to make us believe we're self-sufficient when he knows full well we can't rely on our own ability.

God loves you and wants you home with Him. Heavenly Father made us weak because He knows the only way we will get home to Him is by Christ's power—our inadequacy helps us look to Christ.[3]

ALL HANDS

Due to a childhood accident, my mom's nervous system was a mess for most of her life. Her body often wouldn't do what her brain told it to do. She would have so much pain and pressure in her head, she would sometimes crumple in a heap of sobs. While growing up, I watched her seek the laying on of hands repeatedly.

As a teen, I asked her why she bothered to seek such blessings when it was "obvious" they didn't cure her. Her answer was emphatic: "Those blessings are what get me through!"

I came to believe my mother agreed to endure such agony before she was born—partly to rescue me. I am forever grateful for the lesson she taught me of Christ's grace being enough. She taught me that God's love doesn't mean a total, immediate change of our situation.

By granting us differences and paradoxes that bewilder our intellect and test our fortitude, and by *not* taking away altogether the things that stymie us, God provides a path that helps us look to Christ all our lives.

I finally gained perspective that rather than ignoring my many prayers, God has been granting me grace whenever I sought it—not wholesale change of circumstance, but enough strength to get by while I learned that my "struggle" was a gift that would one day give me profound insights and rewarding relationships.[4]

Opposition helps us learn who we truly are, what we really value, and what we are capable of. My differences from others have taught me to cherish diversity (how much could we learn from clones of ourselves?) and—gradually—to gain empathy for people in trials that I cannot comprehend.[5]

God presents us with an impossible path to convince us that alone, we cannot do what is required to live with Him. Under law, no one but Christ is justified—because no other person is capable of doing all that is required to live with God.[6]

But here is the love and genius of our heavenly parents: Only one of their children needed to fulfill all the requirements of "righteousness." By His merits, we can return home—whole. Remember that justice is dispassionate; it doesn't care from whom the "pound of flesh" is torn, as long as it's paid in full (to borrow from Shakespeare).[7] This morbid thought can bring hope when we consider that Christ's atoning sacrifice not only pays penalties but restores anything we lose.[8]

We qualify for this restoration through covenants. First, we must hope enough that Christ really has such power that we turn to Him constantly and hold out our hands in faith. You may call baptism a "work," but I call it holding out my hands to receive grace. Remember the secret I discovered when I committed to be chaste on my mission? When we promise God sincerely, it doesn't mean we *can* fulfill the covenant, yet God extends Christ's power—grace—to us. I had no idea how I could ever succeed, but my desire was true, so I was given the power to keep my covenant.[9]

I've made covenants in the past and *not* kept them. If I'm honest, I can usually see where the grace extended to me was equal to my minimal desires and sincerity, which were insufficient. Though I didn't realize it at the time and took the credit myself, the success I enjoyed on my mission showed me the power of covenants and grace.

"Impossible" commandments and covenants may be the key to understanding Christ: He asks us to bind ourselves to Him in order to make us the most free; that is, to have the most power and options. Satan "frees" people from rules and standards in order to enslave them to appetites, for the self is never satisfied.[10]

POWERFUL WEAKNESS

I finally grasped through the gift of my addiction that transformative power is not mine. What Satan meant to destroy me, God permitted to be the very instrument that would bring me to His power and to redemption. Had I not been persuaded so completely of my impotence by the chains of compulsive behavior, I may never have truly looked to the only being able to save me and perfect me.

Some might chafe at the idea of personal powerlessness; there's a quote some might cite about the power being in *us* to bring "much righteousness." Yet, note the terminology on *agency*: "Men should be anxiously engaged in a good cause, and do many things of their own *free will*, and bring to pass much righteousness. For the power is in them, wherein they are *agents* unto themselves. And inasmuch as men do good they shall in nowise lose their reward."[11]

Both lines speak of agency or free will being our power. Our power is to *choose* which power moves us. We can steer (though God's better at that too), but we do not power our vessels, just as we do not manufacture the oxygen our body involuntarily takes in from moment to moment. The scriptures universally state that *all* power is Christ's. We either choose Christ's liberating power, or we subject ourselves to the ultimately immobilizing whims of the devil.[12] Our weakness is also a gift that, hopefully, brings us to our Savior.

I GUESS I CONFESS

Recall how for years I did everything I could think of to be free of sexual compulsion—without success. I needed God's power over Satan's chains. Yet, no amount of fasting, prayer, or scripture study was freeing me. As soon as I demonstrated sincerity by doing whatever tiny token God asked of me, I received grace to overcome the compulsion. (In my case, God first asked me to speak not just with Him but also with other people about all my feelings and deeds.) His empowering grace was a first for me, from the time I surrendered my will to the devil via poor choices.

Typically, I felt most comfortable telling other men: a counselor, my bishop, my oldest brother, and twelve-step companions. Confession is an essential, powerful key to freedom. By not being rejected—by being loved in spite of past choices—I felt the new joy of acceptance by men that was not tied to sex. God was meeting my needs and giving me power via my declarations of powerlessness! (I acknowledge that not everyone gets a supportive response from people.)

Honesty not only helps me retain free will, get back on track, and overcome compulsions; it also serves as a kind of insurance *before* a crisis. Confessing desires contrary to my higher goals to another person typically eases temptation's in-the-moment intensity.

No amount of pleading or self-denial will remove our God-given need for healthful connection with others, but honesty with God and others can minimize compulsion.

Scripture study didn't fix things; worship and twelve-step meetings didn't either. But by showing sincerity via *all* these little "steps"—doing whatever I could see to do—I demonstrated that I wanted grace to keep my covenants, and God gave me grace.[13]

It's not our own power that makes us Christlike, able to bear the weight of Father's glory. Alone, we are incapable of something so wondrous. But by putting ourselves in contact with the power of godliness via covenants and sincere reaching, His power is manifest in us.[14]

"Following the Savior will not remove all of your trials," says Dieter F. Uchtdorf. "However, it will remove the barriers between you and the help your Heavenly Father wants to give you. God will be with you."[15]

My life hasn't become carefree; I still have temporal struggles. I'm still required to regularly and healthfully meet my same-sex emotional needs—God isn't taking that responsibility from me, though He is helping me do it by placing amazing people in my path.[16]

God wants us each to feel unable to comply because we each *need* to come to Christ to be saved from sin, death, weakness, and the sins and weaknesses of others that harm us. God loves us *and* has expectations of us. "A God who makes no demands is the functional equivalent of a God who does not exist."[17] Honest accountability with another human being and accountability to God through covenants are true steps to restoring agency and perfecting us.[18]

POINTS TO PONDER

- Opposition helps us learn who we are, what we really value, and what we are capable of. In what ways has opposition helped you know yourself better?

- By giving us "impossible" commandments, paradoxes, and differences—and by *not* taking them away altogether—God provides a path that helps us look to Christ all our lives.
- Paradoxically, Christ asks us to bind ourselves to Him to make us the most free. Satan "frees" people from rules and standards to enslave them to their own desires. How does this relate to the paradox of choice and restriction (in chapter 12), and how does this understanding affect the way you make decisions?
- Everyone needs grace to compensate for our weakness and qualify us to live in glory. We show we want God by trying to keep covenants with Him (accomplished via grace). How can recognizing your weakness strengthen your relationship with God?

NOTES

1. Hank Smith, 2022, (Facebook, April 11, 2022), https://www.facebook.com/photo.php?fbid=559296005557989&set=pb.100044327834890.-2207520000..&type=3.
2. "You're not a hypocrite because you have a bad habit you are trying to break. You are a hypocrite if you hide it, lie about it, or try to convince yourself the Church has the problem for maintaining such high standards. Being honest about your actions and taking steps to move forward is not being a hypocrite. It is being a disciple. . . . [Spend] . . . less time hating [self] for what [you've] done and a lot more time loving

Jesus for what He has done." Bradley R. Wilcox, "Worthiness Is Not Flawlessness," *Liahona*, November 2021, 62.

3. Ether 12:27.
4. 2 Cor. 4:17, 12:9. A family story my mother used to tell about her great-grandmother demonstrates how rather than removing difficulty, Christ's grace often gets us through it one day at a time. Karl Beckstrand, *Agnes's Rescue* (Midvale, UT: Premio Publishing, 2021).
5. 2 Ne. 2:11.
6. Gal. 3:11.
7. William Shakespeare, *The Merchant of Venice* (New York: Gramercy Books, 1997), 223–224. Ultimately, no one will *demand* justice; it would mean a pound of flesh from each of us for harm we've caused, and none of us is without fault. See also Brad Wilcox, *The Continuous Atonement* (Salt Lake City: Deseret Book, 2009) for details on how Christ satisfies justice.
8. Though you may yet be waiting for satisfaction for all harm and loss you've suffered, it is inevitable for those who look to Christ. So, how do the faithful get everything and everyone back that we've ever lost plus more than we can dream of? God's resources are limitless. Any worthy child of His will have access to *everything* (not just temporal things). Christ is worthy—and He's handing out treasures from God's infinite stores to us, who have lost prizes and persons and passion over the course of our lives. He does this because His happiness comes from giving of self to bless others. This is *our* recipe for long-term happiness, too. To gain by giving might appear counterintuitive, but our spiritual self

is infinite (consider our Source); it will *never* run out. We actually increase in glory by giving of ourselves to others (again, in this life, we should also practice self-care). Note the use of the word *restoration* in Acts 3:21, 1: Cor. 15:22 ("shall all be made alive"), and Alma 40 and 41. Some deficiencies "of mortality will be set right in the Millennium . . . the time for fulfilling all that is incomplete in the great plan of happiness for all of . . . Father's worthy children." Dallin H. Oaks, "The Great Plan of Happiness," *Ensign*, November 1993, 94. "That doesn't mean that every blessing is deferred until the Millennium; some have *already* been received, and others will continue to be received until that day." M. Russell Ballard, "Hope in Christ," *Ensign*, May 2021, emphasis added, https://www.churchofjesuschrist.org/study/general-conference/2021/04/28ballard?lang=eng. See D&C 98:3.

9. "In the Lord's own way and time, no blessing will be withheld from His faithful Saints. The Lord will judge and reward each individual according to heartfelt desire as well as deed." Russell M. Nelson, "Celestial Marriage," *Ensign*, November 2008, 94.
10. Luke 7:30; Mos. 18:8–10; Ether 12:27. See Linda K. Burton, "The Power, Joy, and Love of Covenant Keeping," *Ensign*, November 2013, https://www.churchofjesuschrist.org/study/general-conference/2013/10/the-power-joy-and-love-of-covenant-keeping?lang=eng. See also Brad Wilcox, *The Continuous Atonement.*
11. D&C 58:27–28.
12. Matt. 28:18. "I am the vine . . . without me you can do nothing." John 15:5. See also 2 Ne. 2:27–29.

13. "If we love God enough to try to be fully faithful to Him, He will [eventually] give us the ability, the capacity, the will, and the way to love our neighbor and ourselves." Jeffrey R. Holland, "The Greatest Possession," *Liahona*, November 2021, 9. Alma 37:16.
14. 2 Cor. 4:17; D&C 84:20. It's not the putting of the bread or wafer in one's mouth each Sunday that activates covenants; the act alone could be considered as hollow as offering food to idols without sincere reaching to God. We succeed when we sincerely show and say to Him, in essence, "I know nothing I do is sufficient to improve anything, yet I know you have all power. I open my hands to receive the only power that can make me whole."
15. Dieter F. Uchtdorf, "A Yearning for Home," *Ensign*, November 2017, https://www.churchofjesuschrist.org/study/general-conference/2017/10/a-yearning-for-home?lang=eng.
16. Luke 4:18.
17. D. Todd Christofferson, "Free Forever, to Act for Themselves," *Ensign*, October 2014, https://www.churchofjesuschrist.org/study/general-conference/2014/10/free-forever-to-act-for-themselves?lang=eng.
18. See Appendixes and https://PremioBooks.com/joy (or final page QR code) for practical insight on meeting needs and for more tools for regaining/retaining free will.

CHAPTER 14

What If I've Never Experienced Grace?—Higher Paths

"Go out into the darkness and put your hand into the Hand of God. That shall be to you better than light and safer than a known way." [1]

—Minnie Louise Haskins

SINCE I MOVED TO UTAH FROM California, I've encountered people who say, "I want to be happy—and I think God wants that for me too." This is absolutely true.[2] Yet, some continue (unsatisfied) from partner to partner (euphoria to euphoria), seeming to ignore or reject God's guidance on happy human relations.[3]

I've also met LGBTQIA people who have bitter feelings toward the Church of Jesus Christ. I suspect that some didn't have the positive experiences that I've had with Church leaders. I wish that all people had been loved and supported and encouraged as I have been, but I acknowledge that God only has flawed mortals as servants on earth.[4]

To my regret, I began to judge bitter people. I'd ask myself, "How could anyone imagine that God doesn't love them or that His plan for everyone's eternal bliss excludes gays—or that how we feel today represents how we will feel forever?" And I'd wonder, "Have some people really never experienced *any* change of heart or perspective in any area of life?"[5]

Finally, it occurred to me that many people haven't felt, or aren't aware of having, Christ's empowering grace in their lives. As an addict on a fatal trajectory, perhaps I was made to grasp grace (though dimwittedly) because my need was so dire.

Yet, Christ's liberating and soul-altering grace has always been operating in all our lives. He's never withheld it; I just needed to recognize it and discover how it could be a more integral part of my life. I've learned that grace can free me from bondage, give me strength for the day, help me find loving friends, and alter my very nature to be more and more like His. The changes may be small and slow, but I've learned that His grace is available to pull me through every change I'll ever need to make.

Still, the changes I experienced were not the ones I'd expected! I once hoped that God would empower me to avoid every attractive man, limiting my interactions with them to the necessary work for my career and church. Instead, God has helped me improve how I interact with men and *increase* that interaction in healthful ways.

By meeting my legitimate need for male connection, I (with grace) gradually regained rational decision-making power over my social relating and my life. Because my unmet needs were no longer constantly foremost in my mind, all of my human interactions improved. I'm evolving. I'm still bi in orientation, and I'm happy about that. Now, because I am surrounded by affectionate people, I don't go overboard trying to meet those needs for connection. My objective is relating rather than euphoria, though I do get both.

Perhaps some people are experiencing profound disappointment that life isn't unfolding as they anticipated. If this is you, you're not alone![6] While you may have issues with God's timing or methods, I promise that His plans for you are better than what you've had in mind.[7]

Because I've experienced some actual changes (not total, not instant), I have an unshaken conviction of the following:

1. Christ's power to free us from *any* kind of rut, bondage, addiction, habit, routine, family tendency, persecution, oppression, abuse, or actual incarceration;
2. Christ's ability to transform anyone who wishes to be more like Him;
3. Christ's motivation—it isn't vanity; it's to grant us joy. He offers grace to everyone, with no respect for family or other status. I have no doubts about His motives or ability to make me a "new creature"

> (while respecting the wonderful, unique things that will always make me me).[8]

As I recognized the gift of grace working in me, my judgments of others began to melt. It became clear that someone who hasn't felt the enabling and transformative power of grace might feel discouraged and helpless in the face of the Lord's high standards. If you don't know that the Savior will give you a ladder and spot you while you ascend, it's easy to resent the prize on the impossibly high shelf!

God will not cease to speak truth just because it makes some people uncomfortable. He reveals truth with the *intent* that we be uncomfortable with our own self-sufficiency; His celestial standards are meant to make us lose hope in our own power—but never to make us lose all hope! God's standards help us grasp our need for a Savior who transforms sinners into saints. The standards are real. The impossible task of meeting them *alone* is not![9]

Since our birth as spirit children of God, choice and consequence have been emphasized and fought for. Though agency means we're free to experiment, we can avoid a lot of grief by *not* experimenting where God has already given instruction. Our all-powerful Savior can liberate any (willing) person from anything, but experimenting with potentially addictive things is dangerous, not because God isn't able to save but because a person enmeshed in addiction may not seek liberation. Perhaps such a person won't feel worthy of liberation or won't believe that Christ *can* free them from such strong chains. Beliefs impact behavior, but behavior can also build or erode belief. But be assured, no matter our own vacillations, the Savior and His grace are available to us. There will never *not* be a Liberator![10]

SOME GRACE TAKES TIME—THE PATH OF PATIENCE

It's a paradox, but the ultimate free expression of one's true self can only happen with discipline. Even so, "Discipleship is not about doing things perfectly, it's about doing things intentionally."[11]

Grace is not typically a quick fix and requires patient faith. It is also not inherent in us—we must constantly look to Christ and remain connected to Him throughout this life and beyond. Still, I ache with anyone who sees only permanence in mortal circumstance and life's paradoxes. I lament any notion that would limit God's infinite power to multiply our options and enjoyments.

There are many things I do not know, but I know that everyone who desires to be like our Heavenly Father can, over time, attain those characteristics via Christ's grace.[12]

> *"[God] is aware of each of us and our needs. . . . The Lord's timing is different than ours. Sometimes we seek for a blessing and set a time limit for the Lord to fulfill it. We cannot condition our faithfulness to Him by imposing upon Him a deadline for the answers to our desires."*[13]
>
> —Ulisses Soares

POINTS TO PONDER

- Though God will always respect individual choice, we miss blessings by presuming to know better than God how connectedness and happiness are attained. How does your agency work with God's will?
- Mortal circumstances and paradoxes have never been eternal destinies. Christ has all power, but He exercises it on His own timetable. How does this perspective inform your decision-making?
- We can't meet God's expectations alone. Yet, His consistent high ideals for us help us come to the Savior, and He transforms sinners into saints. How does this understanding of the Savior free you to be more yourself than ever?
- The ultimate expression of true self can only happen with discipline. Still, "discipleship is not about doing things perfectly, it's about doing things intentionally." How do intent and discipline help reveal your true self?

NOTES

1. Minnie Louise Haskins, "The Gate of the Year" (London: Hodder and Stoughton, 1940).
2. "While everyone has access to Christ's *total* transformative and enabling power, remember: The commandments of God are 'strict' because His kingdom and its citizens can stand only if they consistently reject evil and choose good,

without exception." D. Todd Christofferson, "The Love of God," *Liahona*, November 2021, 16–17. "Jesus clearly understood . . . that there is a crucial difference between the commandment to forgive sin (which He had an infinite capacity to do) and the warning against condoning it (which He never ever did even once)." Jeffrey R. Holland, "The Cost—and Blessings—of Discipleship," *Ensign*, May 2014, 8.

3. "The proud wish God would agree with them. They aren't interested in changing their opinions to agree with God's." Ezra Taft Benson, "Beware of Pride," *Ensign*, May 1989, https://www.churchofjesuschrist.org/study/ensign/1989/05/beware-of-pride?lang=eng.
4. Clearly, there are people who show little tolerance (and sometimes hatred) for differences. (I believe this is a fear of the unknown and that if we knew how enriching differences can be, we'd seek out people different from us daily—and love sharing with them.) "Imperfect people are all God has ever had to work with. This must be terribly frustrating to Him, but He deals with it." Jeffrey R. Holland, "Lord, I Believe," *Ensign*, May 2013, https://www.churchofjesuschrist.org/study/general-conference/2013/04/lord-i-believe?lang=eng. See Appendix F (online: https://PremioBooks.com/joy) for more insights.
5. See endnote 5 in chapter 6.
6. Jer. 29:11. God can and does make good come from even tragic events (ever know an athlete who, due to an injury, ended up in their ideal career?). Still, His power and genius don't equate to license on our part (why choose unnecessary pain and consequences?). Take heart; *most* choices are a matter of individual taste and are not governed by law

or commandment. I'm finally realizing there are no totally negative experiences; even the worst circumstances teach me and make me wiser. How you live affects—for good or bad—your beliefs. Some people fail to follow God's will; then, because blessings don't come as anticipated, they condemn His work as false. The Lord has addressed this. See D&C 3:3, 58:32–33, 130:20–21, 136:42.

7. D. Todd Christofferson, "Our Relationship with God," *Ensign*, May 2022, https://www.churchofjesuschrist.org/study/general-conference/2022/04/41christofferson?lang=eng. Jer. 29:11; Rom. 8:28; Ps. 32:8, 33:11; Prov. 3:5–6, 16:3–4, 16:9; 1 Cor. 2:9.
8. "Christ's version of unity is about togetherness, not sameness." John K. Carmack, "Unity in Diversity," *Ensign*, March 1991, 7–9.
9. "God's intent is not to break us but to redeem us. He does not want us to be brokenhearted but to have broke hearts and contrite spirits so that He can take the reins of our lives and guide us with His love to receive all of His promised blessings." L. Todd Budge, "'Broke' Hearts and Contrite Spirits," BYU devotional, February 2, 2021, https://speeches.byu.edu/talks/l-todd-budge/broke-hearts-contrite-spirits/; Isa. 1:18; Micah 7:19; Alma 33:16. See Mos. 7:33; 2 Ne. 26:22, 28:22.
10. "Jesus came and spoke unto them, saying, All power is given unto me in heaven and on earth." Matt. 28:18. "Finally, be strong in the Lord and in the strength of His might." Eph. 6:10. See also Isa. 40:29; Luke 5:17; 1 Cor. 2:5; Eph. 1:19–21, 2:8–9; Phil. 4:13; 1 Pet. 1:3–5; 2 Ne. 2: 8–9; Mos. 2:21; "30 Bible Verses about the Power of Christ," Knowing Jesus, n.d., https://bible.knowing-jesus.com/topics/The-Power-Of-Christ.

11. Dieter F. Uchtdorf, "Your Great Adventure," *Ensign*, December 2019, https://www.churchofjesuschrist.org/study/general-conference/2019/10/43uchtdorf?lang=eng.
12. Jeffrey R. Holland, "The Greatest Possession," *Liahona*, November 2021, 9.
13. Ulisses Soares, "Take Up Our Cross," *Ensign*, November 2019, 115, https://www.churchofjesuschrist.org/study/general-conference/2019/10/55soares?lang=eng. "The joy we feel has little to do with the circumstances of our lives and everything to do with the focus of our lives. When the focus of our lives is on . . . Jesus Christ and His gospel, we can feel joy regardless of what is happening—or not happening—in our lives. Joy comes from and because of Him." Russell M. Nelson, "Joy and Spiritual Survival," *Liahona*, November 2016, 82–84.

CHAPTER 15

What's Good About Attraction to One's Own Sex?—Your Unique Path

To choose is our gift and our right—sealed on the family of Adam and Eve via Christ's atoning sacrifice. Because our freedom is bought with a price (as are we),[1] it is our responsibility to choose well. I hope to have opened many options to you.

CAN COMPETING DESIRES AND OPTIONS BE a good thing? Remember how I said it would be worthwhile to ponder why a loving Father in Heaven would allow His beloved children to experience difficulty. I have seen time and again, in my life and in the lives of others, God take something Satan meant for harm and turn it for our good. This book highlights several such scenarios. More than likely, you have seen God work this way in your experience too.

Have you ever read or watched a story of a mortal who is granted omnipotence? If it's a well-thought-out portrayal, it will show how overwhelming and potentially destructive such power can be to the holder. I believe we are given challenging differences throughout our lives to grow. By navigating the consequences of our own and others' choices, we learn increasing patience, compassion, self-control, and love for ourselves and others. Eventually, when we're with God, we'll be more prepared to shoulder the responsibility of being like Him, of having knowledge (power) like His.[2]

I've heard addicts say they are grateful for addiction—as am I, for bringing me to my Savior—but for years, I couldn't see a *single* reason to be grateful for my attraction to men. That is no longer the case.

Despite (or, perhaps, partly due to) my attraction to men, the young me was a homophobe—seeing gays as less valuable than other people and, therefore, seeing myself as less legitimate than other people. Something astounding happened in my earliest nonsexual embraces a few years ago: One man I was holding had characteristics that were not attractive to me, but while holding him, I felt an overwhelming love, and I realized it was not my own love that I felt for him, but God's love for him.

Somehow, because I felt love for that gay man, I was able to feel love for myself, a man also attracted to men. I saw our value—his and mine—as children of God. As soon as I loved me as I am, God's love for me burst through to my soul—as though I had been holding it at bay all my life. I always knew in my mind that God loved me, but I had imagined He couldn't love this part of me, so I hadn't allowed myself to feel His love until that moment. I don't believe God was ever withholding love; it's just that I couldn't feel what I hadn't accepted.

Today, I'm pleased with who I am *and* with my feelings. I know, not only in my mind but also in my heart, that God loves me. He has always seen my life with an attraction to men and has always lovingly had plans for this to become one of the best parts of my journey.

Child advocate Susan H. Porter says, "Sometimes we mistakenly think that we can feel God's love only after we have followed [Christ]. . . . God's love, however, not only is received by those who come to [Him] but is the very power that motivates us to seek [Him]."[3]

Not only does God love part of me and of you, He loves all of us *and* our differences. That doesn't mean He wants us to remain static or unchanging; I am saying He has a purpose for *all* the differences we compare ourselves to others with. He sees what differences can do toward granting us empathy and perfecting each other mutually.[4]

Perfection and glory have never meant homogeny. I won't debate whether God makes people gay—I only declare that He knows beforehand who will feel what and that the plan He makes with each of us includes using *any* of our differences to strengthen us and to bless us and others.

Today, thanks in part to ill health and family shortcomings (things Satan meant to squash me), I enjoy ongoing and deep connection, love, and acceptance with outstanding people. I've learned I can love many people deeply without shortchanging others—and without possessiveness, guilt, or dependence.

I am grateful for my attraction to men. If offered a pill to become one hundred percent "straight," years of deliberation would fail to bring me to a decision. I'm not saying that being heterosexual is less than, but knowing what I know about myself and the experiences I have with others because of my feelings, I believe I'm richer for the poignant separations, connections, and values I've gained because of same-sex attraction. Some of my experiences have been so profound, I doubt I could have had them under other circumstances. Difficulty and all, I would choose my own experience.

PATHS OF STARS

A big reason people are attracted to people is to experience deep and lasting connection (in a variety of forms and relationships). But look at any relationship around you; it seems there must be divine intervention to achieve relational peace, let alone bliss. While God doesn't give instructions about every little thing, what are your chances for long-term relationship happiness without paying attention to the wisdom He *has* shared on human relations? Whether or not you marry, will you invite God into your relating choices, now and forever?[5]

I don't condemn anyone for disagreeing with God's blueprint for relationship happiness at first glance or with my postulations on same-sex relating. For some time, my own feelings and actions were not in conformity. But I'd only seen part of the blueprint, so I didn't yet believe in God's plans for same-sex happiness! I've learned that Heavenly Father truly loves us all, that He is mistaken on nothing, and that He really has power to help each of us grow to be like Him.

Understanding the undiluted love of our heavenly parents, the sacrificial love of Christ, and their plan for our lasting happiness gives us a lens through which to understand all that they do. Through this lens, we can more easily receive and value unchanging doctrine—while embracing differences, change, and unpredictability in mortality.

Knowing of this love and that God will never force us, that everything He does is for our benefit, and that all will be made right—and more than fair—I can receive life's highs and lows and not borrow grief from calamities that will, likely, never be.

An example of how we might embrace differences and difficulties for a higher purpose can be seen in my South American mission experience. Even with my illness and the impact it has had on the rest of my life, if I had to choose between all I gained on my mission *or* having great health, without hesitation, I would keep my treasured missionary experiences and relationships. Even knowing beforehand how serving would affect my health, I would do it again. If the church called me on a mission today, I'd say yes in an instant. I'd be the slowest, happiest missionary on earth! My passport is still current.

YOUR UNIQUE PATH

Agency and justice, good and evil, light and dark are real paired principles or opposites, but not everything is binary, and *many* things fall outside of right or wrong. There are usually countless options, though seeing them may require contemplation. Most choices, even mistakes, are *not* sins. An ancient Hebrew prophet taught, "Where there is no law given there is no punishment; and where there is no punishment there is no condemnation."[6]

I believe that human relationships are eternal. Some people say they don't want a God that separates families in the next life, but the many mansions and kingdoms of heaven are not holding cells! Just because some people won't be able to endure God's or Christ's immediate radiance doesn't mean that family members won't see or interact with each other or that ongoing development won't happen!

I hope all people who feel attraction to their own sex—or who feel any isolating difference—can learn its positive purpose and optimal expressions. I hope we find profound connections with others who feel "different" and gratitude for the enrichment that differences can bring. If you truly believe God has always known all things, you will grasp that there is a benefit in everything. While I don't pray that people be transformed into heterosexuals, I *do* pray that each of us may find grace and freedom forever from *any* idea or situation that reduces choices.

The body of Christ needs you. I envision a non-distant day when pure same-sex affection is common in the church—and no longer an indicator of sexual immorality anywhere in Western culture—and when even those who *are* sexual with same-sex partners are loved and encouraged along the gospel path. I see it happening now. If you don't see it, perhaps you're not looking for it. I often find what I look for.

I've been in Latter-day Saint worship services with a man's arm around me—and we were warmly welcomed. My dad's never-married cousin and her female companion of decades both just passed away. They loved each other deeply and came together to all family gatherings; we loved them dearly. Active in church, they traveled, made and kept covenants with God, advised and empowered countless students, and died with a solid hope of eternal glory with God and each other.

There are many gay couples that give up sex (or choose never to be sexual) and discover supernal connection that seems to only deepen. I've heard of gay men who come back to church (sometimes because they can no longer perform sexually). They're not necessarily abandoning their partners, yet these men die keeping all covenants. It seems that God draws people to Him in a variety of ways.

KEEP A WEATHER EYE TO THE CHART ON HIGH AND GO HOME ANOTHER WAY [7]

The wise men, after visiting the child Jesus, were "warned of God in a dream that they should not return to Herod," instead, "they departed into their own country another way."[8]

Educator and youth leader Michelle Craig spoke of ancient missionaries sent to teach a king:

> Aaron was teaching the king of the Lamanites, who wondered why Aaron's brother . . . had not also come to teach him. "And Aaron said unto the king: Behold, the Spirit of the Lord has called him another way." . . .
>
> Each of us has a different mission to perform, and at times the Spirit may call us in "another way." There are many ways to build the kingdom of God as covenant-making, covenant-keeping disciples of Jesus Christ. . . . You can receive personal inspiration and revelation, consistent with His commandments, that is tailored to you. You have unique missions and roles to perform in life and will be given unique guidance to fulfill them.[9]

Noah and Moses each tackled a large body of water differently. Craig says, "They each received personalized direction, tailored to them, and each trusted and acted. The Lord is mindful of those who obey and . . . will prepare a way for us to accomplish the thing which he [commands]." Note that she says "*a* way"—not "*the* way."

> Do we miss or dismiss personal errands from the Lord because He has prepared "a way" different from the one

> we expect? . . . Trust God to lead you, even if that way looks different than you expected or is different from others.
>
> [People] come in many shapes and sizes, but "all are alike unto God." . . . No matter who you are or what you're dealing with, you are invited to the Lord's table.
>
> As seeking and doing the will of the Father becomes the cadence of your daily life, you will, of course, be led to *change* and repent.
>
> The Church . . . is built on the foundation of . . . discovering what the Lord would have us do, and then acting on that direction. Each one of us, regardless of age or circumstance, can strive to seek, receive, and act. As you follow this eternal pattern ordained for our day, you will draw nearer to Jesus Christ—His love, His light, His direction, His peace, and His healing and enabling power.[10]

Believe that, alone, *no one* can be whole. There is only one path to our Father in Heaven, and that is through Jesus Christ. But—thankfully—there are *multiple* paths to Christ! I have presented some ways to meet needs and follow Christ.

The future of this planet is glorious. Your future is glorious. You may have believed that your circumstance proved God was against you, but it could actually be evidence that He is working for your good. He has prepared paths for you to find lasting, loving relations now and forever. I believe most everyone can find those paths with grace.[11] I've long been certain that heaven would be a place of love and affection with those dearest to me. Apparently, I'm already there.

NOTES

1. 1 Cor. 6:20; Matt. 20:28.
2. Knowledge is indeed power. See Luke 12:44, 13:28, 16:19–31. These verses (along with the meaning of Abraham's name) imply that Abraham is now in a glorified, omnipotent state (though not necessarily worshipped. Again, I know of *no* doctrine that says any but the Father, Son, and Holy Spirit will be worshipped). See also Rom. 8:17; Phil. 2:9; 2 Tim. 4:8; Rev. 3:21, 21:7.
3. Susan H. Porter, "God's Love: The Most Joyous to the Soul," *Ensign*, November 2021, 34.
4. Our differences make us *beautiful.* Anomalies like the Dead Sea or the Grand Canyon attract intense interest and wonder. The world would be very boring if everyone were the same.
5. Read these verses in the context of one another. (Some Bible verses thought to be against homosexuality in fact speak against pedophilia; yet, many scriptures warn against sexual acts between adults of the same sex—for our own happiness.) Gen. 1:22, 1:27–28, 2:24, 19, 37–38, 39:1–18; Exod. 20:14; Lev. 18:20–22, 20:10–13; Num. 25:1; Deut. 5:18; 1 Kings 14:24; 2 Kings 23:7; Ps. 51:10, 119:9; Prov. 31:10; Matt. 5:27–28, 15:19, 19:4–9; Mark 10:2–12; Acts 15:19–20; Rom. 1:18–32, 2:22, 13:13; 1 Cor. 7:2–9, 5:9–11, 6:9–11, 6:18–20, 10:8; 1 Thess. 4:3; 1 Tim. 1:8–11; 2 Tim. 2:22; Titus 2:4–12; Eph. 5:3, 28–31; 1 Pet. 2:11; Jude 7; Rev. 2:14, 9:21, 14:1–5; Jacob 2:28; Alma 13:28, 39; D&C 121:45.

6. 2 Ne. 9:25. I still struggle with binary thinking!
7. James Taylor and Tim Mayer. "Home by Another Way." Track 8 on Never Die Young. Country Roads Music/Manor House Music, 1988, compact disc.
8. Matt. 2:12.
9. Michelle Craig, "Spiritual Capacity," *Ensign*, October 2019, 21. See also Alma 24:27.
10. Craig, "Spiritual Capacity," 21.
11. Jer. 29:11; Ps. 32:8, 33:11; Prov. 3:5–6, 16:3–4, 16:9; Rom. 8:28; 1 Cor. 2:9. For more information and resources on same-sex relating (regardless of orientation), overcoming old ways of thinking or compulsions, and increasing options, see: https://PremioBooks.com/joy.

Key Points

I'VE COVERED LOTS OF MATERIAL IN this book, and many ideas here may be new to you, or maybe they're old ideas from new angles. Whether you're queer or questioning yourself or you want to better understand a loved one, I hope this book is helpful to you. In that spirit, I've provided this list of key points to help you get a better grasp of what I've tried to share. Whether you've read the whole book or not, this summary of key points should be useful to you.

- I believe that relationships can be eternal and the source of our greatest joys. Yet, we need God's help for long-term relationship bliss (regardless of sexual orientation).
- Awareness of options increases power and satisfaction. By presenting multiple paths, I don't mean to imply that each is equally desirable—or that all are harmless.
- Sexual orientation is not contagious, a defect, a sin, a mortal choice, or an act of rebellion. We can exert influence over feelings, but often, we simply feel what we feel.

- God loves LGBTQIA persons! God doesn't just accept queerness; it is part of His plan for mortal happiness. It's not mere tolerance—neither is it acceptance of gay sex as a positive expression of gayness. God has always known what we would experience. His plan has always been that we could benefit from it all.
- Agency and opposition have always existed. While God respects individual choice, we miss blessings by disregarding God's counsel for happy relationships. Consequence is not a construct that God can wave away.
- Few choices are binary. There are infinite ways to be human, let alone LGBTQIA. There may be better ways to love and be loved (regardless of orientation) than the standard ways the world signals.
- People attracted to their own sex will likely remain so attracted, at least while in mortality, for wonderful purposes. People of the same sex are designed to love each other powerfully—without possessiveness, guilt, or dependence—and *with no loss of love for anyone* (our source of love is infinite). While same-sex love isn't exclusive, it's possible that the person you have the deepest connection to—now and in eternity—is the same sex as you.
- Like our need for oxygen, same-sex emotional needs are God-given and ongoing. They must not be ignored. God can help us fill needs—but He won't remove them.

- Emotional connection is a need. As good as it is, sexual euphoria is not love and doesn't satisfy true need. Confusing transitory euphoria for love is almost a guarantee that a person will fall out of "love" due to the fleeting nature of euphoria.
- Sex in itself isn't bad—but inappropriate sex, heterosexual or otherwise, disconnects us from the joy of union (and can be torture to escape; wanting more always leads to wanting more).
- While any sexual activity has the potential for selfishness, sexual stimulation between people of the same sex appears to result in emotional distancing—even for those who wait until they're in love. Few people have experienced the profound connection that can endure between people of the same sex who avoid being sexual with each other.
- Emotional needs can manifest as sexual desire, like feeling hungry when you're dehydrated. By neglecting true emotional connection, the feeling of neediness persists, regardless of how much sex one has. Meeting emotional needs healthfully can illuminate true needs, open previously unimagined relational possibilities, and might also reduce compulsive behavior.
- Celibacy and sobriety *don't* necessarily mean healthful or whole. A person can be sexual and chaste, and a person can be celibate yet unchaste.

- Authenticity and chastity are rooted in seeing self and others as divine. Most people prefer loving to being loved; giving love is deeply fulfilling.
- Hiding our differences and difficulties can lead to destructive isolation. Honesty with trusted people can promote growth, bring liberating grace, and save us before a fall.
- Most choices, even mistakes, are not sins. Competing desires can help us learn who we are, what we value, and what we are capable of. Individual worth doesn't change.
- The surest way to reduce options is to reject any constraint. Principles and boundaries can increase options, while having all you want can lead to bondage.
- The libido can be an indicator of how well or how poorly we are meeting emotional needs. You can work with your libido instead of battling it or being its slave. When emotional needs are met the libido becomes very calm; images and fantasy—even face-to-face propositions—lose their magnetism.
- Willpower cannot be our ultimate source of strength. Grace is more than God's love or mercy; it's divine transformative power which He extends to us through the atoning sacrifice of Jesus Christ (2 Cor. 12:9; Ether 12:27).
- To relate with those of one's sex in a lasting fulfilling way, a person must gain their own conviction that:

1. Your attraction to those of your sex is part of God's plan for your happiness.
2. Non-sexual same-sex connection fulfills and creates lasting bonds.
3. Same-sex sexual relations erode union.

- True connection and euphoria aren't mutually exclusive. Physical arousal is a normal biological reaction in human relating; it doesn't necessarily mean sex is on the agenda.
- Conversation is a super way to meet God-given emotional needs—even without touch.
- Naked holding or indulging in same-sex sexual thoughts each distract from true connection.
- Same-sex bonds can be repaired. There are happy gay couples who are no longer (or never were) sexual, yet have been bonded for decades.
- Non-sexual same-sex connecting is not a technique to endure temptation—it satisfies God-given needs, reduces frustration, and brings joyful relationships that can last forever.
- No mortal can complete you. True intimacy can't be attained if one is out of sync with self or with God. Your God-need is legitimate; the ultimate expression of true self can only happen with Him.
- We all need grace to compensate for weakness and qualify us to live in glory. Christ asks us to bind ourselves to Him to maximize our freedom and

options. Satan "frees" people from rules and standards to enslave them to their desires. We show we want God by trying to keep covenants with Him (accomplished via grace).

- Mortal circumstance and paradoxes have never been eternal destinies. We can't meet God's expectations alone. Yet, His consistently stated high ideals for us help us come to the Savior, and He transforms sinners into saints. Christ has all power, but He exercises it on His own timetable.
- Perfection and glory have never meant homogeny. God loves us and sees what differences can do toward empathy and perfecting each other mutually. God loves us and has expectations of us. Trying counts with God.
- You can receive individually tailored guidance (consistent with God's commandments) via the Holy Spirit to fulfill your unique mission.
- A circumstance you believed proved God to be against you, might actually be evidence that He is working for your good. Your most rewarding relationships may not be the one(s) you're currently in, pursuing, or think you're missing. They might result from the loss of relations or expectations previously held as important. Seeing abundant options might require modification to current notions.
- I believe everyone will be ecstatic with their gender

in eternity and that relationships will be beyond satisfying—and we needn't wait until then. Whether it is by a change in us and our desires (*every* person needs change) or by receiving something better than we ever hoped for, no one in God's kingdom will feel denied, cheated of, or lacking anything (Ps. 23:5).

EPILOGUE

More Than 2 Paths to Relating with a Gay Loved One—For Families of LGBTQIA Persons

(Please see Key Points and chapters 2, 6, 7, 10, 11, 14, and 15.)

YOU MAY JUST HAVE LEARNED THAT a loved one is LGBTQIA; your head may be swimming. It's normal to feel inadequate to even respond. One of the first feelings may be guilt—please surrender that to God and let His love and peace fill you. You may have been taken by surprise, but He *never* is.

May I offer you my assurance that regardless of what you or your loved one might feel at present, these differences—like all differences—are gifts to bless us. When I finally figured out how these kinds of differences enrich my life, I was overwhelmed with how much God loves me and how exquisite the gift of difference is. I would *never* alter what differences have brought me.

Like this book's title suggests, you don't have to choose between promoting unhealthful choices (which exist for everyone, regardless of orientation) and being hateful. There are far more loving and helpful responses.

WHEN LOVE ISN'T LOVE

Some of the worst pain in our lives can come from those closest to us—both via rejection and via too much "support" at the sacrifice of good judgment and even truth.[1] Some of us have heard of someone being disowned and/or kicked out of the house for being gay or of someone's partner being ignored or insulted by family. This is not loving one's neighbor (it's certainly not loving one's "enemy"; this is your loved one/a fellow child of God!).

You are *not* condoning sin by loving your LGBTQIA family member. Of course, you can still have expectations for behavior as long as they live in your home, just as you would for any family member. No family member should attack or demean your faith (and no one should demand that family choose between their faith and a family relationship). But you are *not* denying your faith by loving your LGBTQIA family member; you are living it.

Christian faith asks us to love and respect all people—including your loved one's significant other. You are *not* offending God by saying, "God loves you and I love you," for He loves *all* of us on our unique paths.[2]

While the appendixes that follow offer specific supportive steps and resources for making good choices, here are some thoughts to expand your options and, hopefully, those of the people dear to you.

If the LGBTQIA individual is your child (or a child in your care), it's important to teach them resilience and to stand up for self, even with physical self-defense (hoping it won't be necessary). All bullying—psychosocial and physical—is to be taken seriously. If your child's bullies physically attack four or five at a time, as mine did, self-defense is moot. As soon as you're aware of a situation, *immediately* address it with teachers, youth leaders, administrators, law enforcement, and other authority figures who can help, and work with them toward resolution. Your child may not be the only victim. However, if the problem isn't handled immediately, get your child *out* of that environment, even if it is a "worship" environment!

Perhaps you cannot afford a more structured school or other environment; perhaps you don't have the luxury of home or private schooling (*truly* lamentable). If your child must remain in a public school or another less-structured environment, be persistent in exploring options for other classes, even other schools or districts. Do not back down until there is a place where bullying isn't tolerated.

If your child's school teaches human development or health courses (what was once called "sex ed"), advocate for age-appropriate curriculum that teaches inclusion but is balanced as to sexual expressions (hollow, isolating, unrestrained expressions must be countered by instruction on consequences and on expressions that foment lasting, boundary-respecting bonds that cherish all involved [see chapter 10]). Ideally, this guidance should come from *you*.[3]

Protect your child against those who (even in the name of love and support) too quickly or ill-advisedly encourage ideologies and choices that are harmful. Some individuals and families confuse divine confirmations of God's love (for them, for each person, for who we are right now) to be a divine waiver of God's expectations and standards. Some parents try so hard to support or not offend their children that they never challenge their child on any idea. Rather than be concerned for their child's *lasting* happiness, they try to put their child's comfort (or their own status with their child) above truth or above God for fear that their child might not like them. Sacrificing truth in the name of love is neither helpful nor loving.

I believe God gave us differences so that we would learn from one another—and spread our love broadly, as He does. Of course, we sometimes bite our tongues (wisely) when someone isn't in a place to healthfully hear truth (and for better long-term relations). That situation is different from pretending that something harmful isn't harmful—or from outright encouraging the harmful things! To paraphrase myself, if a person hasn't experienced firsthand, long-term, sexually monogamous happiness in a same-sex union, perhaps they shouldn't encourage what they don't know is or isn't good for people.[4]

Unconditional love never equates to license—nor can it make consequences evaporate.[5] Unconditional love simply means that the object of our love can never do anything that would make us stop loving them, and this fact should be expressed!

When faced with something difficult, we can lower the standard, or we can try our best. Again, trying counts with God, and His grace empowers us to accomplish things we couldn't on our own.[6] I think the best thing one could do for an LGBTQIA child is to live the gospel of peace, which, along with love, includes real trust in the Lord and His grace, His power, His love, and His timing.[7]

Additionally, protect your child against those who would paraphrase or spin spiritual discourse as being hateful (unless preachers use epithets or condemn people rather than of ideas). Be wary of "advocates" or "bridge builders" who demean or who think condescension is a loving way to alter opposing positions.

Most parents want life to be fair for their kids. Yet, some parents accuse those who speak God's timeless ideal of sexual purity and morality of being haters. Given the options, described in earlier chapters, for supernal same-sex relationships now and in eternity, why might some parents become incensed when God's law of chastity is reemphasized? This kind of sensitivity isn't advocacy. It facilitates self-deception and is misleading to kids and other impressionable people who are trying to identify who they are and what's important.

The devastating part of such sensitivity is that some well-meaning people could be contributing to someone's discouragement and despondency, even a child's. If a public or religious figure discusses options for LGBTQIA people that include chastity, some parents (regardless of how the message is articulated) hear a bigot oppressing or condemning their child.[8] Some people paraphrase messages in such a light. Negative paraphrasing or message-spinning can cause LGBTQIA people to avoid hearing the *original* messages—meant to bless them with increased choices, were they heard directly from their authors. Does negative interpretation help a person avoid overwhelm and the feeling of rejection? I think it can foment it—perhaps more so than typically loving, supportive statements by faith leaders earnestly encouraging contentment by mapping out positive choices.

I acknowledge that some leaders and laypeople have been (and even are today) bigoted and ignorant.[9] While change *is* needed in the church and in society at large, as charity director Sharon Eubank says, "I believe the change we seek in ourselves and in the groups we belong to will come less by activism and more by actively trying every day to understand one another."[10] What good does it do to interpret a well-meaning message as being hurtful or hateful or to tell someone you love how they should feel or react? Telling another what to think is an effort to limit their choices. There are ways to support a loved one without abandoning trust in God, His words, or His servants.[11]

Help kids find peace with who they are and with where they are in their lives' journey: not shame, not pride, but *peace.*[12] If you hear a statement on LGBTQIA issues that rubs you the wrong way, perhaps the best thing to say to your LGBTQIA child is "I love you, and I know that God does too."[13]

With regard to gender identity, keep fluidity in mind. I believe that even intersex individuals (hermaphrodites) at some point attain a clear understanding of their eternal gender identity—despite initial doubts. I believe that in the eternities, *everyone* will be clear on their identity and will be ecstatic about it. Keep in mind, many people—including me—have experienced fluidity regarding physical attraction. Fluidity (even over decades) in gender identity is not uncommon.[14]

Encourage your child to be patient and prayerful in self-discovery.[15] Even attractions unfold at different rates—and many early attractions aren't physical (see Appendix B). Yes, promise to keep your mind open, but wait until your child's brain is capable of adult reasoning before taking permanent steps, like agreeing to or facilitating surgery or a limiting philosophy or treatment that would be painful (or next to impossible) to undo. It is vital to evaluate *long-term* experiences and attitudes of many people who have experienced various options in this area.[16]

Awareness of mental health is critical:

> Dr. Michelle Cretella, executive director of the American College of Pediatricians, told *The Christian Post* that [a]

> study "confirms what no one disputes: Namely, that youth who identify as LGBTQ have higher rates of mental illness leading to a greater risk of life-threatening behaviors." But contrary to what these authors conclude, Cretella said, there is "no evidence that 'destigmatizing efforts' will solve the problem, because there is no evidence that the higher rates are due primarily to stigmatization." She pointed out that Sweden is among the most LGBT affirming nations in the world, yet, LGBT mental illness and suicide rates in Sweden are just as dramatically elevated relative to the general population.[17]

"Improved mental health contributes to improved spirituality," says Steven J. Lund, "but research is showing the reverse is also true: improving spirituality improves mental health."[18]

I'm convinced that our choices help—or retard—our ability to grasp what brings lasting happiness; choices like those God would make open our eyes and hearts more to the perspective and happiness He has. Contrary choices delay our becoming like Him, postpone our even seeing the difference between a momentary comfort and enduring joy. In my experience, choices that lead me away from becoming like my Heavenly Father slow my development (at minimum, they delay my happiness). Regardless, we must be patient with ourselves, God, and others.[19]

Like others with same-sex attraction, I have been promised that if I keep my covenants, no blessing will be denied me, but I will always have a choice. I have every reason, plus a lot of scriptural basis, to believe that profound relationships are the norm in heaven—perhaps especially between people of the same sex—but that doesn't have to be the entire picture.[20] Whether or not you believe that family units remain intact in eternity, we are promised that those who attain God's immediate presence will have every attribute that Christ has; essentially, there will be no one with whom we won't want to associate. (Again, *everyone* needs to change to live with God, but no one will be forced in anything. See chapter 5.) Whether or not one marries, I'm confident that no one's social sphere in heaven need be limited to a spouse.[21]

It is unhelpful to say that I or others will never want traditional marriage; it's comparable to saying that heavenly dessert will taste like raspberries to heterosexuals and stale bread to gays (and totally incongruent with the generous nature of the Chef). I'm contented now with my relationships and the possibilities—and choices—ahead.

FOR SPOUSES OF LGBTQIA PEOPLE

If you are married to someone attracted to their own sex, it can be overwhelming—even bewildering. But know this: Your opposite-sex spouse's sexual orientation has nothing at all to do with you. Neither is any addiction of theirs your responsibility. However, a spouse's attitudes about sex and intimacy—physical and emotional—may play a role in whether their partner seeks physical gratification outside the marriage. Bear in mind that the gender of a cheating spouse's other partner(s) is not a reflection of your fully realized masculinity or femininity.

My friend Tim is a bi man married to a heterosexual woman. After explaining to Tim's wife that he and I never get sexual (or naked) but that he and I share laughter, deep conversation, and affection, her concerns about Tim's needs and moral behavior have been greatly assuaged.

Isolation and ultimatums are unlikely to improve the situation. Just as no argument or threat of loss prevented me from acting on my addiction, no fear, heartbreak, pleading, or withdrawal on the part of a spouse will eliminate a person's legitimate needs. While such expressions might *temporarily* alter behavior, we're not discussing being denied wants (like wanting a cookie), but legitimate needs. These are needs God himself won't remove—needs that must be met healthfully, in ongoing ways, or they become masters in undesirable ways (think Donner Party). Please see chapters 7, 10, and 11 on reducing risk via healthful same-sex relating. As we seek healthful ways to satisfy our needs for human connection, I know that God can help each of us through our fears and troubles as we look to Him.

If one or both spouses have not kept their covenants, counseling (individual and couple) is a helpful first step. I hope this book provides positive insight as to true needs and how to meet them. It is critical that both partners in a marriage understand such needs and meet them healthfully.

NOTES

1. Every human love, at its height, has a tendency to claim for itself a divine authority. Its voice tends to sound as if it were the will of God Himself. It tells us not to count the cost, it demands of us a total commitment, it attempts to over-ride all other claims and insinuates that any action which is sincerely done "for love's sake" is thereby lawful and even meritorious. That erotic love and love of one's country may thus attempt to "become gods" is generally recognized. But *family* affection may do the same. So, in a different way, may friendship. Lewis, *The Four Loves*, 7, emphasis added.
2. Matt. 5:44. See also George, "The Philosophical Basis."
3. You may be concerned that your child might be indoctrinated into an LGBTQIA life. I have good and bad news: My experience is that—regardless of sexual experimentation or propaganda—a person eventually settles into what they know deep down reflects who they are (and their first guess is sometimes wrong; see Appendix B). Some people might be in their 30s or 50s before they really feel comfortable with who they are and what they are about! Experimentation, fluidity—even indoctrination—aren't uncommon, but don't let the notion that each person eventually figures self out make you neglectful, letting your child stumble unattended. Indoctrination might not affect them permanently, but premature sexual activity—and its frequent companions of sexual confusion and addiction—are topics far too complex and difficult for a child to deal with alone (apparently the brain is not fully developed until we're in our twenties). (FYI: Many kids who were molested by someone of their

own sex never become gay, and many who weren't molested do.) Do everything you can to help them avoid these bumps. Parents: Six or seven years is *not* too early an age to begin to discuss sex and personal boundaries with your child. Even younger children can grasp basic body safety and personal boundaries. And be completely on top of what others might be teaching your kids. See "At What Age Is the Brain Fully Developed?" Mental Health Daily, n.d., https://mentalhealthdaily.com/2015/02/18/at-what-age-is-the-brain-fully-developed/; The Alcohol Pharmacology Education Partnership, "Content: Brain Maturation Is Complete at about 24 Years of Age," Duke University, n.d., https://sites.duke.edu/apep/module-3-alcohol-cell-suicide-and-the-adolescent-brain/content-brain-maturation-is-complete-at-about-24-years-of-age/.

4. Some people behave as if love and truth are mutually exclusive—and loyalty should trump truth (because truth can sometimes be painful). Of course, we sometimes hold our tongues when someone isn't in a place to healthfully hear truth; yet, true loyalty doesn't withhold truth long-term, and it never misleads or lies. (Truth doesn't need us to shout or drone it incessantly.) Even if, for better long-term relations, we presently avoid certain topics, our pretending that something harmful isn't harmful—or encouraging something harmful—is neither love nor loyalty! Some people think loyalty is blind; they support poor choices because of *who* is making them. But devotion to truth is a better measure of loyalty: If someone truly loves you, they likely won't say that everything you do is good.

5. "We have to be careful that love and empathy do not get interpreted as condoning and advocacy, or that orthodoxy and loyalty to principle not be interpreted as unkindness or disloyalty to people. As near as I can tell, Christ never once withheld His love from anyone, but He also never once said to anyone, 'Because I love you, you are exempt from keeping my commandments.' We are tasked with trying to strike that same sensitive, demanding balance in our lives." Jeffrey R. Holland, "The Cost—and Blessings—of Discipleship," *Ensign*, May 2014, 8.
6. "With the gift of the Atonement of Jesus Christ and the strength of heaven to help us, we can improve, and the great thing about the gospel is we get credit for trying, even if we don't always succeed." Jeffrey R. Holland, "Tomorrow the Lord Will Do Wonders."
7. Hebrew prophet Lehi didn't leave the tree of life to persuade his family to come to it. He remained at the tree (committed to God above all else) and invited his family from there. How can a person hope their children will follow the iron rod of God's word (or be confident of making it back oneself) if they have left it?
8. Isa. 29:21.
9. "Imperfect people are all God has ever had to work with. This must be terribly frustrating to Him, but He deals with it." Jeffrey R. Holland, "Lord, I Believe."
10. Sharon L. Eubank, "By Union of Feeling We Obtain Power with God," *Ensign*, November 2020, 55–57.
11. Here's a talk affecting families with LGBTQIA members (that some may not have heard due to paraphrasers): Russell M. Nelson, "The Love and Laws of God," BYU devotional,

September 17, 2019, https://speeches.byu.edu/talks/russell-m-nelson/love-laws-god/.

12. Rather than emulate shame—or pride—perhaps peace and trust in God should be our outlook. Some parents want to be dragon-like in defending their kids (the sentiment is understandable). Still, recalling one symbol of Christ (the meek lamb) might help us maintain an open mind—and have more influence with our children—long-term.
13. Trust that the purpose of "many mansions" in heaven is *not* to keep people from their loved ones and that there is no permanent hell (unless you want that). See chapter 5 and D&C 19.
14. Please see chapters 6 and 7 on fluidity. While growing up, I had massive crushes on girls, though I was slow to experience physical attraction to them. See Gospel Topics, "Understanding Yourself," The Church of Jesus Christ of Latter-day Saints, https://www.churchofjesuschrist.org/topics/transgender/understanding?lang=eng
15. There's nobody exactly like you, and if you're bold enough to inquire [with God], I believe you'll be swamped with impressions about your purpose—more than you ever thought possible. Most of all, I hope you know there is no category that can hold you except that of being a child of the eternal God. The Lord sees you. You're not invisible to Him. He loves your efforts that no one else may see. You're valuable, and He treasures you in all your quirks and individuality. If you trust your life to Him, His hand will guide you every step of the way until you are happy and at peace with all the desires of your heart. Sharon Eubank, "A Letter to a Single Sister."

16. See Ester di Giacomo et al., "Estimating the Risk of Attempted Suicide Among Sexual Minority Youths: A Systematic Review and Meta-analysis," *JAMA Pediatrics* 172, no. 12 (December 2018), 1145–52, https://doi.org/10.1001/jamapediatrics.2018.2731; Donald Antrim, "Finding a Way Back from Suicide," *The New Yorker*, August 9, 2021, https://www.newyorker.com/magazine/2021/08/16/finding-a-way-back-from-suicide; Susan Berry, "Science Says Transgender Hormones and Surgeries Do Not Prevent Suicides," *Breitbart*, June 30, 2021, https://www.breitbart.com/politics/2021/06/30/science-says-transgender-hormones-and-surgeries-do-not-prevent-suicides/; Kiley Crossland, "Sex Change Regret Silenced," *World*, October 6, 2017, https://world.wng.org/content/sex_change_regret_silenced; John Sexton, "One Woman's Story of Becoming a Trans Boy and Later Detransitioning," Hot Air (blog), February 21, 2022, https://hotair.com/john-s-2/2022/02/21/one-womans-story-of-becoming-a-trans-boy-and-later-detransitioning-n450114; Lizette Borreli, "Transgender Surgery: Regret Rates Highest in Male-to-Female Reassignment Operations," *Newsweek*, October 3, 2017, https://www.newsweek.com/transgender-women-transgender-men-sex-change-sex-reassignment-surgery-676777.
17. Leah MarieAnn Klett, "Gay, Transgender Youth at 'Significantly Higher Risk' of Suicide Than Heterosexual Peers: Study," *Christian Post*, December 18, 2018, https://www.christianpost.com/news/gay-transgender-youth-at-significantly-higher-risk-of-suicide-than-heterosexual-peers-study.html.

18. Steven J. Lund, "How the Children and Youth Program Strengthens Families," *Liahona*, March 2022, https://www.churchofjesuschrist.org/study/liahona/2022/03/united-states-and-canada-section/how-the-children-and-youth-program-strengthens-families?lang=eng. See also Sheldon Martin, "Strive to Be—A Pattern for Growth and Mental and Emotional Wellness," *Liahona*, August 2021, https://www.churchofjesuschrist.org/study/liahona/2021/08/strive-to-be-a-pattern-for-growth-and-mental-and-emotional-wellness?lang=eng; Erich W. Kopischke, "Addressing Mental Health," *Liahona*, November 2021, 37–38; Reyna I. Aburto, "Thru Cloud and Sunshine, Lord, Abide with Me!" *Ensign*, October 2019, 58; Carolyn McNamara Barry et al., "Profiles of Religiousness, Spirituality, and Psychological Adjustment in Emerging Adults," *Journal of Adult Development* 27 (September 2020): 201–11, https://doi.org/10.1007/s10804-019-09334-z; Alen Malinovic et al., "Dimensions Of Religious/Spiritual Well-Being in Relation to Personality and Stress Coping: Initial Results from Bosnian Young Adults," *Journal of Spirituality in Mental Health* 18, no. 1 (2016): 43–54, https://doi.org/10.1080/19349637.2015.1059301; Shannon Gwin et al., "The Relationship between Parent–Young Adult Religious Concord and Depression," *Journal of Spirituality in Mental Health* 22, no. 1 (2020): 96–110, https://doi.org/10.1080/19349637.2018.1549524.
19. Mark 10:30; 1 Sam. 18:1–5, 20:16–17, 20:41–42, 23:16–18; 2 Sam. 1:26. "In the Lord's own way and time, no blessing will be withheld from His faithful Saints. The Lord will judge and reward each individual according to heartfelt desire as well

as deed." Russell M. Nelson, "Celestial Marriage," *Ensign*, October 2008, 94.

20. The implication that some blessings are reserved only for exalted male-female couples is a huge indicator—given what we know of God's love, grace, and equanimity—that we will, at some point, want what He offers (not just go along with it!).
21. "And that same sociality which exists among us here will exist among us [in heaven], only it will be coupled with eternal glory." D&C 130:2; Moses 7:63.

APPENDIX A

Suggestions for Coming Out—If You Choose

DON'T FEEL PRESSURE TO COME OUT. Pray about when, how, and with whom to share your feelings. Follow good impressions. Consider whom you want to tell and why (whom you are attracted to is not necessarily everyone's business). If you don't want the whole world to know, the person or people you come out to must be trustworthy; you should have a good sense that they love you and are capable of keeping confidences. Therapists, counselors, and clergy are obligated to keep your personal information confidential unless they find you might hurt yourself or others (legally, they have a duty to report that).

Have a support system beyond those you plan to tell. This can be a therapist, clergy member, support group (most are anonymous), or other safe professional outside your family and friends.[1] There are LGBTQIA hotlines as well. (See the QR code at the end of the book.)

Consider outcomes. If you are financially dependent on your parents and there's a possibility that they might withdraw support or kick you out, it may be wise to wait until you have a backup plan for where to go and how to support yourself.

Neeral Sheth, a psychiatrist specializing in LGBTQIA health at Rush University, "advises against publicly coming out if you're just beginning. 'You might see celebrities coming out publicly through a social media post or a press conference, but I don't recommend doing anything like this—at least not until you have a core group of people that you know will support you 100%.' Social media can also be risky, as people you don't know well may make negative comments. And if even if you do know them, Sheth says that you should be prepared for people to have different reactions to your news, especially if they did not expect it."[2] Others, wanting to be supportive, may naively encourage you toward choices that may be destructive to you.

When it's the right time, a script may help you avoid misunderstandings. It may be good to prepare the person you're telling. Ask for what you need:

- "I'd like to speak with you tonight."
- "I want to tell you something; will you listen?"
- "Would you have time to talk? I have something I'd like to share with you; it may be difficult to hear."
- "I need you to keep this between us until I'm ready to share with others."

Speak what's in your heart. Here are some starting options:

- "You're important to me; I want you to know that I'm gay/bisexual/pansexual/lesbian/transgender/asexual/queer. This means that I (am attracted to ___/identify as ___)."
- "I've thought about this for a while and feel that . . ."
- "I'm not attracted to . . ."
- "This is hard for me" or "This is very personal."
- "It's been difficult hiding my true feelings."
- "I haven't mentioned this before because . . ."
- "I want to be honest with myself and with you because it's difficult to accept love or feel connection while wondering whether people would love or accept this part of me."
- "I'm sharing this because I love you and hope we can still have a good relationship."

Prepare for questions. These options allow a loved one space and time to digest:

- "I'd like to talk more later, when you've had some time to think."
- "I'm happy to share what I can" or "I don't want to talk about details; I just wanted you to know."
- "I hope you will always accept me."
- "I'll try to answer your questions, but maybe not all at once."
- "I love you. Thank you for . . ."

If things don't go well, remember a person's *initial* response my not be what they intend. You may need to reassure them, set a boundary, or pause the conversation. Things may improve with time. Here are a few suggestions for how to handle a negative reaction:

- "I know you're concerned/angry; I still love you."
- "I'm still the same person you've always known."
- "I don't want to fight; I hope you'll change your mind."
- "I'm going to take a break, but I will be back at . . ."
- "I need to stop for now; perhaps we can talk later."[3]

NOTES

1. Support for LGBTQIA people: https://www.northstarlds.org/; suicide hotline: 1-800-273-8255; https://www.focusonthefamily.com/get-help/counseling-services-and-referrals/.
2. MK Manoylov and Zil Goldstein, "How to Come Out to Your Friends, Family Members, and More—And How to Make Sure It's Healthy and Safe for You," Insider, January 20, 2021, https://tinyurl.com/ycka492y.
3. See "Coming Out to Your Parents," Strong Family Alliance, 2017, https://www.strongfamilyalliance.org/how-to-come-out-to-parents/.
4. Information enhanced with ideas from LDS.org, Asha French, Caitlin Ryan, Family Acceptance Project, and Bianca Salvetti, "How to Talk to Your Child Who Is Questioning or Identifies as Lesbian, Gay, Bisexual, Transgender, Queer or Asexual (LGBTQA)," RN Remedies (blog), Children's

Hospital Los Angeles, June 24, 2016, https://www.chla.org/blog/rn-remedies/how-talk-your-child-who-questioning-or-identifies-lesbian-gay-bisexual-transgender.

APPENDIX B

How to Respond When a Loved One Comes Out to You (& What Not to Do)

IN ADDITION TO THIS SECTION, YOU may find it helpful to review the list of Key Points as well as chapters 2, 6, 7, 10, 11, 14, and 15.

Coming out may be a time of complex emotions and reactions for all involved, but a simple expression of love has the power to calm and reassure. If you don't know what to say, you can always say, "I love you, and God loves you." You don't have to understand your loved one's situation to express your love for them.

While it is typically unproductive to tell a child they are simply going through a phase when they come out to you, discovering identity *is* a process—and what one thought was set in stone can evolve. It has for me and others.

My friend Jay came out to his parents as gay when he was a young adult. He laughs because, contrary to what he predicted, his stern dad—not his sweet mom—took the news in stride (his mom had to go compose herself in the other room). What *none* of them anticipated was that a while later, Jay realized that he didn't want a gay partnership (at least not in the common definition); he discovered he is asexual! "Questioning" is a real state.

Patience with self, loved ones, and God is always a good thing. Here are some other ideas to help you and your loved ones:

- Listen. Ask questions.
- Thank them for telling you. Assure them, "I will always love you."
- Believe that your loved one can have a happy life as an LGBTQIA person (and that gender and sexual orientation are only a part of a much broader identity and life).
- If you need time to digest the news, assure your loved one that you love them and ask for some time to take it in. Follow up—and don't delay this! Check in every once in a while.
- If you learn about your loved one's same-sex attraction secondhand, don't take it personally.
- If you react poorly, apologize.
- Where comfortable for both, give affection. Be courageous. Some teens give a vibe that they don't want hugs, but they often really do.

- Stand up for your loved one if anyone (including family) is disrespectful. You don't have to advocate a certain lifestyle—but every person deserves love and respect.
- Research different perspectives and data—don't rely on your loved one to be your only source of information.
- If your loved one is living with you, don't alter your standards for them. Be sure they understand your expectations, and encourage wise and healthful choices. If the person is a minor, regular conversations about sexual morality are essential—regardless of orientation (see chapters 5–8 and 10–15). These conversations don't have to be formal but can be in the course of other activities.[1]
- Always get permission before sharing about your loved one with someone else.
- Where appropriate, humbly share your experiences and challenges with others.
- Welcome your loved one's partner or LGBTQIA friends to your home and to family gatherings. This is not a surrender of your personal moral standards; it is loving one's neighbor (and, hopefully, retaining positive influence with your loved one).
- If your loved one expresses any suicidal thoughts or desires, or a desire to harm themselves, get them professional help.[2]
- Try to honor a transgender (or any) person's wishes regarding name choice. It shouldn't be difficult to

use whatever name a person chooses. If you cannot bring yourself to call your trans loved one their preferred pronoun, ask if they'd be okay with you using terms like you/*they/their*. Be patient with each other, as it takes time to replace old habits with new ones.

- Continue to pray for and serve your loved one. The least productive prayer is "Why?" A close second is "Please take this away right now." The most helpful prayers are the following: "How can I help? How can I be the support my loved one needs? How can we learn from this?"
- Encourage loved ones to confide in honest people. A person's devotion to truth, not just love, is an excellent measure of potential loyalty and sound counsel.

QUESTIONS YOU MIGHT ASK

- "What does gay (or bi, etc.) mean for you?"
- "What has it been like discovering this?"
- "How are you feeling now?"
- "How can I best support you?"

THINGS TO AVOID

- Don't bemoan a "sad" situation (verbally or otherwise), and don't ignore or pretend like you didn't hear the information. Don't name-call or criticize gays or queers in general.
- Don't feel guilty. If the loved one is your child, remember that while you may not have been a

perfect parent, your parenting likely has nothing to do with your child's sexual orientation or gender identity.

- Don't assign stereotypes to your loved one (e.g., that they likely have great fashion sense, have mechanical or sports ability, or should be a natural dancer).
- Don't exclude your LGBTQIA loved one from activities or family gatherings. (Don't worry what other people might think of you!) Don't pressure your loved one to tell certain people.
- Don't insult, ignore, yell, hit, or physically hurt your loved one or pressure them to be more (or less) masculine or feminine. Don't restrict your loved one's access to rational friends, resources, activities, or organizations for fear they might act on gay feelings.

AVOID SAYING

- "Don't you think you should try dating the opposite sex?"
- "Are you sure?" (Though, keep my friend Jay in mind!)
- "I knew it all along." (Maybe you did, but so what?)
- "Don't you know what the scriptures say about this? God doesn't want gays. He punishes them." (This is inaccurate and harmful.)
- "This is probably just a phase." (That's possible, but when earlier pains or changes arose for your loved one, did you ignore those?)

- "Please don't tell anyone else." That's your insecurity talking; this is about your loved one, not you.
- "I hope you won't be flamboyant about this." (You allow others free expression; allow your loved one to determine how they express themselves.)

CONSIDER

- Does this knowledge change the deep emotions you felt when this person entered your life or the feelings you've had for this person to this point?
- You will never regret showing love or saying "I love you" to a loved one. You will never regret listening and trying to understand.
- It's natural to grieve. Do you feel your dream of the "perfect" family slipping away? Do you fear losing a close relationship? Are you afraid your loved one won't be treated with kindness? These feelings are natural. There is no shame in grieving.
- Blaming yourself or others is neither warranted nor helpful.
- Believe that your loved one can have a happy life as an LGBTQIA person and that gender and sexual orientation are only a part of a much broader identity and life.

(Information enhanced with ideas from LDS.org, Asha French, Caitlin Ryan, Family Acceptance Project, and Salvetti, "How to Talk to Your Child.")

APPENDIX C

How to Support Parents & Families of LGBTQIA People

DON'T BE SILENT OR PULL AWAY; don't ignore; don't speculate regarding the family member's worthiness or future. See chapters 1, 2, and 6 before making any comments about causation or choice or change. Don't worry what your association with LGBTQIA people might imply to others; model fearless love!

Try not to make assumptions about anyone's sexual orientation. Don't lecture or simplify or brush LGBTQIA issues aside. Don't make assumptions about how the family member is living—what they are doing or not doing—alone or with others. Don't raise eyebrows when LGBTQIA people are given jobs in church; many may be keeping covenants better than you.

Visit. Offer empathy, love, and support. Reach out to the family member, too. Give hugs. Tell them you love them. Educate yourself on related topics. Ask sincere questions in an effort to understand and then listen. Try to imagine how these families might feel.

ASK

- "How is _____ ?" (If the loved one is a child, ask about *all* their children.)
- "How can I help you and your family member know you're all loved?"
- "Is there something that might help your loved one feel more welcome at church/school/etc.?"

SAY

- "I love your family member and your family; we want to be friends with you!"
- "We need LGBTQIA people as part of the body of Christ. Each is important and valuable!"
- "I love and accept your family member just as they are!"
- "I may not know what it is like to be in your shoes as the parents/family of a gay individual, but I would really like to understand."
- "I never want to say the wrong thing or anything hurtful, so please tell me if I do."
- "Your family member is welcome in my home."
- "I won't try to give unsolicited advice, but I'm

always here if you need to talk."

- "No judgment here!"
- "I want your family member to be healthy and happy. I will try to support in healthful ways."

(Information enhanced with ideas from LDS.org, Asha French, Caitlin Ryan, Family Acceptance Project, and Salvetti, "How to Talk to Your Child.")

APPENDIX D

How to Help Someone with Questions About God & LGBTQIA Topics

THE BOOK YOU'VE JUST READ IS a resource for anyone with questions about how God feels about LGBTQIA persons or who has concerns about living Christ's gospel as an LGBTQIA person. If someone you love struggles with questions, be loving, open, and long-listening. Assure them of your love for them and of God's love for them.

Questions are how we get answers and grow. God doesn't mind sincere questions; He possesses all truth, and He desires that *everyone* have as much truth as they will receive (James 1:5). My experience is that if I am patient and sincere in my seeking, answers and perspective gradually unfold to me, but I must accept God's timing. Neil L. Andersen promises, "Honest questions . . . will be settled with patience and an eye of faith." (Neil L. Andersen, "The

Eye of Faith," *Ensign*, May 2019, 36.) Of course, there are some things I still wonder about—but I *know* God loves me and has a plan for my happiness, and this is an excellent lens through which to view those things I have yet to receive answers for (1 Ne. 11:17).

One word of caution: If your actions create dissonance within you or your beliefs, you can improve your behavior to match your beliefs, or you can alter your beliefs (what you believe is right or wrong, for example) to align better with how you are living (there are likely more options, but these two do for my point). How you live affects—for good or bad—your beliefs. Acts of faith strengthen faith. Some people fail to follow God's will; then, because blessings didn't come as or when anticipated, they condemn His work and word as false. (See D&C 58:32–33, 130:20–21, 136:42.)

For more information and resources on same-sex relating (regardless of orientation), eternal doctrine versus ever-changing policy, overcoming old ways of thinking or compulsions, and increasing options, see: https://PremioBooks.com/joy (QR code below).

RECOMMENDED READING

C. S. Lewis, *The Four Loves* (Boston, New York: Mariner Books, 2012)

Meghan Decker, *Tender Leaves of Hope: Finding Belonging as LGBTQ Latter-day Saint Women* (Springville, UT: Cedar Fort, 2022)

Chip Heath and Dan Heath, *Decisive: How to Make Better Choices in Life and Work* (New York: Crown Business, 2013)

Brad Wilcox, *The Continuous Atonement* (Salt Lake City: Deseret Book, 2009)

Colleen Harrison, *He Did Deliver Me from Bondage* (Hyrum, UT: Windhaven, 2006)

Gary Chapman, *The 5 Love Languages: The Secret to Love that Lasts* (Winston-Salem: Northfield Publishing, 2014)

Sexaholics Anonymous (Brentwood, TN: Sexaholics Anonymous, 1984)

Juli Slattery, *God, Sex, and Your Marriage* (Chicago: Moody Publishers, 2022)

Karl Beckstrand, *The Joys of Male Connection* (Midvale, UT: Paths Press, November 2022)

OTHER POPULAR TITLES by Karl Beckstrand:

The Joys of Male Connection: Building Lasting Satisfying Relationships—Regardless of Sexual Orientation

The Bridge of the Golden Wood: A Parable on How to Earn a Living

No Offense: Communication Guaranteed Not to Offend

To Swallow the Earth: A Western Thriller

Horse & Dog Adventures in Early California: Short Stories & Poems (with Ransom Wilcox)

Bright Star, Night Star: An Astronomy Story

GROW: How We Get Food from Our Garden

Agnes's Rescue

Anna's Prayer

Ida's Witness: The True Story of an Immigrant Girl

Samuel Sailing: The True Story of an Immigrant Boy

Crumbs on the Stairs – Migas en las escaleras: A Mystery

4 Spanish Books for Kids

Gopher Golf: A Wordless Picture Book

Bad Bananas: A Story Cookbook

She Doesn't Want the Worms

Muffy & Valor: A True Dog Story

Share these award-winning titles with other readers: **PremioBooks.com**

To the Reader

I HOPE YOU FOUND THIS BOOK TO be helpful. There is a secular version of this book entitled: *Abundant Paths*. Feel free to connect with me on LinkedIn.com/in/karl-beckstrand or https://www.facebook.com/KarlBeckstrand.AuthorSpeaker. I'd love it if you'd leave a sincere review wherever fine books are sold—and, of course, spread the word!

BONUS MATERIAL:

www.ingramcontent.com/pod-product-compliance
Lightning Source LLC
Chambersburg PA
CBHW031538260326
41914CB00039B/1996/J

* 9 7 8 1 9 5 1 5 9 9 1 5 7 *